Southern Cooking

by Mrs. S. R. Dull

(Abridged Version)

GROSSET
GOOD LIFE
BOOKS

PUBLISHERS • GROSSET & DUNLAP • NEW YORK
A FILMWAYS COMPANY

Illustrations by Lauren Rosen.

Contents

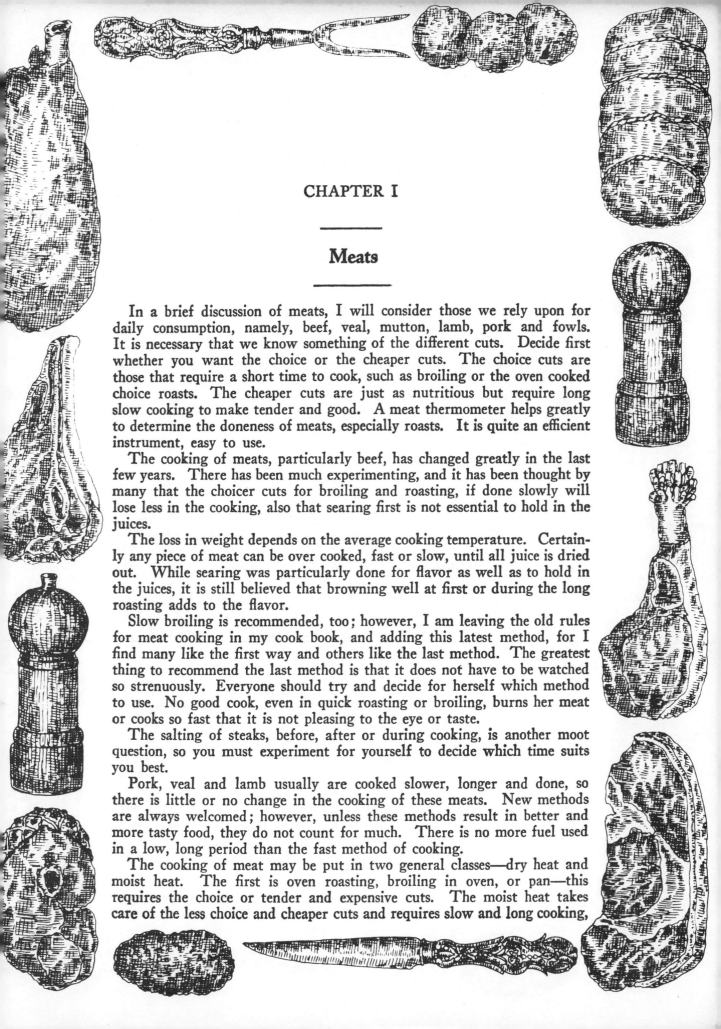

CHAPTER I

Meats

In a brief discussion of meats, I will consider those we rely upon for daily consumption, namely, beef, veal, mutton, lamb, pork and fowls. It is necessary that we know something of the different cuts. Decide first whether you want the choice or the cheaper cuts. The choice cuts are those that require a short time to cook, such as broiling or the oven cooked choice roasts. The cheaper cuts are just as nutritious but require long slow cooking to make tender and good. A meat thermometer helps greatly to determine the doneness of meats, especially roasts. It is quite an efficient instrument, easy to use.

The cooking of meats, particularly beef, has changed greatly in the last few years. There has been much experimenting, and it has been thought by many that the choicer cuts for broiling and roasting, if done slowly will lose less in the cooking, also that searing first is not essential to hold in the juices.

The loss in weight depends on the average cooking temperature. Certainly any piece of meat can be over cooked, fast or slow, until all juice is dried out. While searing was particularly done for flavor as well as to hold in the juices, it is still believed that browning well at first or during the long roasting adds to the flavor.

Slow broiling is recommended, too; however, I am leaving the old rules for meat cooking in my cook book, and adding this latest method, for I find many like the first way and others like the last method. The greatest thing to recommend the last method is that it does not have to be watched so strenuously. Everyone should try and decide for herself which method to use. No good cook, even in quick roasting or broiling, burns her meat or cooks so fast that it is not pleasing to the eye or taste.

The salting of steaks, before, after or during cooking, is another moot question, so you must experiment for yourself to decide which time suits you best.

Pork, veal and lamb usually are cooked slower, longer and done, so there is little or no change in the cooking of these meats. New methods are always welcomed; however, unless these methods result in better and more tasty food, they do not count for much. There is no more fuel used in a low, long period than the fast method of cooking.

The cooking of meat may be put in two general classes—dry heat and moist heat. The first is oven roasting, broiling in oven, or pan—this requires the choice or tender and expensive cuts. The moist heat takes care of the less choice and cheaper cuts and requires slow and long cooking,

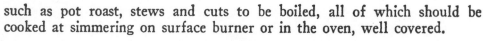

such as pot roast, stews and cuts to be boiled, all of which should be cooked at simmering on surface burner or in the oven, well covered.

BEEF

Beef should be bright red, with fine streaks of fat through the meat, and plenty of firm fat around the outer edge.

A four pound pot roast, shoulder cut or a chuck roast will require two or three hours of slow cooking, while the prime rib, which we consider our most choice roast, will cook in an hour or an hour and a half according to whether you wish it rare or done. I allow twenty minutes per pound after searing. A prime rib roast, less than four pounds, is not apt to be very juicy because it will be so thin the juices will escape.

By searing the roast first the juices are kept in. Even the stews should be seared or browned, thus making a rich gravy both in color and flavor.

Steaks cut an inch or more thick are more satisfactory. Broiling a steak is simply searing first one side then the other until as done as desired.

The round of beef makes an excellent swiss or smothered steak, a meat loaf or individual meat balls, but I do not consider it good for roast.

In my recipes I have tried to make very plain directions for the best and most generally used cuts.

VEAL

Veal is used more during the summer months. Many think because veal is young beef, that it is much easier to cook. This is not true. Veal must be well cooked to bring out the best flavor and nutritive value. The meat should be firm and pink. The cuts are much the same as lamb, there being the chops, cutlets, roast, and stew.

Calf liver is now considered very nutritious. Sweetbreads from veal and lamb are quite a delicacy. Brains from veal are considered more delicate than beef brains, but are not as firm. I prefer beef brains for croquettes or for using for creamed dishes.

MUTTON AND LAMB

In large markets mutton and lamb are always to be found. Spring lamb and baby lamb is usually plentiful during the spring and summer months.

Mutton and lamb should be well scrubbed before cooking. The outside skin or membrane, known as the fell, often gives an objectionable flavor and for this reason some people do not care for this meat. Remove the skin or fell from lamb chops before broiling. Larger pieces, however, should be scrubbed and for this purpose I use a little cooking soda, wiping the meat thoroughly afterwards. The various cuts are: steaks, chops, cutlets, breast, shoulder, leg o' lamb and stews.

PORK

Pork being rich with fat is used freely during cold weather and sparingly in warm weather. In addition to the chops, loin, ham and shoulder, it

furnishes spare ribs, backbones and a choice piece of lean meat called the tenderloin, which is most delicious when broiled thoroughly and served very hot.

Pork may be roasted, boiled, broiled, fried or stewed, and should always be cooked thoroughly. During the winter season pork has always been consumed very freely throughout the South and Southerners enjoy the "hog killing" season, which, in addition to providing the cuts already mentioned, furnishes material for pork sausage, cracklin' bread, liver pudding and hoghead cheese.

FOWL

Of course I could not write a Southern cook book without mentioning fried chicken, although under the head of fowl comes duck, geese, turkeys, pigeons, squabs, guineas and, of course, the popular domestic chicken.

The South is noted for its fried chicken, which nowhere else seems to be quite so good or quite so deliciously prepared. Chicken pie and smothered chicken are two other popular dishes calling for young chickens, weighing from 1½ lbs. to 2 lbs. However, during the season, broiled chicken seems to be a well-liked dish in the South. Broilers usually weigh from ½ lb. to 1 lb.; larger than that are not considered choice. Baked chicken, which calls for the grown hen, is used mostly during the winter, with various dressings and sauces.

FISH

A more general use of fish would tend to decrease the cost of living. Fish, in its food composition, is very similar to beef and contains many valuable nutrititive properties.

The popular belief that fish is a good brain stimulant has been disproved by research authorities, as it has no more phosphorus than lean beef. It is however, an easily prepared and digested protein food.

The digestibility varies with the different kinds of fish. As a general rule fish of fine texture is more easily digested. Smoked and dried fish is not as digestible as the fresh fish.

Both fish and shellfish abound in our Southern waters.

BEEF AND VEAL RECIPES

Standing Prime Rib Roast

Select a standing prime roast which is well trimmed with ribs cut to desired length. Save trimmings for stock and gravy. A piece of fat should accompany each roast. Wipe and scrub rind to remove any bad flavor from hanging. Sprinkle well with flour, and dot each cut side with pieces of fat.

Place under blaze or in hot oven to sear well, turning and browning the cut sides. When seared reduce heat to medium (350 degrees) and cook 20 minutes to the pound for medium rare, longer for well done, and less for very rare. Do not cover. Add no water. There should be enough

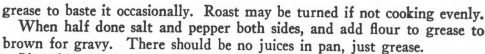

grease to baste it occasionally. Roast may be turned if not cooking evenly.

When half done salt and pepper both sides, and add flour to grease to brown for gravy. There should be no juices in pan, just grease.

If cooking is too slow or pan covered, juice will flow, otherwise juices stay in meat. Do not stick fork in choice part as this also allows the juices to flow.

To Make Gravy

Bones and trimmings from a roast should be put into cold water (covered well) and boiled to make stock. The usual roast and trimmings will make about 2 cups of gravy.

For thickening gravy use 3 tablespoons flour to 1 cup stock.

Remove roast from pan and pour off all grease except just enough to mix with flour. Rub smooth, and add stock from trimmings. Stir and blend all together and strain. No grease should be evident on top of gravy. It requires more flour to thicken when it is browned than when left white.

Prime Roast Rolled

Have butcher bone and roll roast. Cook same as a standing roast. Make gravy same also.

Pot Roast

Select a roast of the cheaper cuts of meat, wipe well and remove any objectionable part. Place in a pot or heavy sauce pan and sear well on both sides. Sometimes it is necessary to rub a little grease over it. The heat should be great to sear well and quickly to prevent the juices from flowing.

When searing is done reduce heat, cover and start to cooking slowly.

It is better to rest the meat on a trivet to prevent scorching, the meat being heavy will press tightly on bottom of pan causing no juice or liquor to be there.

It will require from 2½ to 3 hours to cook a five pound pot roast. The secret of a good pot roast is long, slow cooking. If cooked too fast a little water may have to be added; otherwise there will be sufficient juice supplied for the cooking.

To make gravy, remove excess grease, thicken with white or browned flour, add water and seasoning and cook until as thick as wanted.

Pot Roast With Potatoes

Cook roast as directed above, add peeled Irish potatoes, about 45 minutes before serving, or long enough to cook the potatoes (potatoes should be of uniform size), before making the gravy.

An Oven Pot Roast

Prepare roast by wiping with a damp cloth. Place in roaster and sear in hot oven or under blaze until well browned on both sides. Salt, pepper and season with anything desired. If potatoes are wished, peel and place

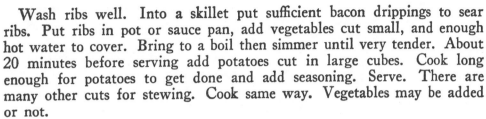

around roast. Place on cover, lower heat, and cook slowly until roast is done at 275°. No water is added at all. With slow cooking there will be sufficient juice or gravy. The gravy may be thickened or not.

Beef Stew

2 lbs. short ribs of beef	4 medium size Irish potatoes
1 onion	Water for stewing
1 carrot	Salt and pepper to season
1 green pepper	

Wash ribs well. Into a skillet put sufficient bacon drippings to sear ribs. Put ribs in pot or sauce pan, add vegetables cut small, and enough hot water to cover. Bring to a boil then simmer until very tender. About 20 minutes before serving add potatoes cut in large cubes. Cook long enough for potatoes to get done and add seasoning. Serve. There are many other cuts for stewing. Cook same way. Vegetables may be added or not.

Broiled Steak

Select a choice cut and have it one inch thick or more. Wipe with damp cloth and remove any objectionable skin or gristle. Clip edge to prevent curling.

Place steak on a broiling pan and put under blaze as near as possible not to touch blaze or heat unit. Cook about 3 minutes, turn, broil the other side, turn again, repeat until as done as wanted.

Remove to a hot platter, add salt, pepper and melted butter. To make gravy add 2 or 3 tablespoons water to the pan and drippings, pour over steak.

To broil satisfactorily requires a hot pan, hot broiler and HOT fire. Leave oven door open and the steak will not catch on fire. About 12 minutes will be required to broil medium done.

The broiling pan, with rack, slides in and out. Pull out to turn steak, push back quickly to prevent getting cold. Never salt or add butter while cooking. Large or small steaks may be broiled this way.

To Pan Broil

Use a heavy fry pan or griddle and have VERY hot.

Prepare steak as for oven broiling, place on sizzling hot pan, turn every 2 or 3 minutes until as done as desired. No grease is used. Sometimes the skillet is rubbed with a piece of steak fat to prevent sticking too much.

Never cover any meat that is being broiled as this draws out the juice, A hot skillet and frequent turning holds juices in. Add salt, pepper and butter after it is on hot platter. Broil any meat the same.

To Plank a Steak

Have all vegetables cooked, seasoned and hot ready to dress the plank.

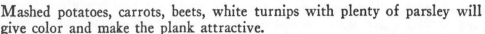

Mashed potatoes, carrots, beets, white turnips with plenty of parsley will give color and make the plank attractive.

Prepare steak 1 inch or more thick the same as for broiling. Place on broiling pan and broil one side thoroughly. Remove steak and place cooked side down on hot, buttered plank. Place plank on pan to handle easily. The edge of plank left exposed beyond the steak must be covered with a light coating of wet salt to prevent burning. Run pan, plank and all in oven very near the blaze and broil. No turning is necessary. When well browned remove, brush and wipe salt from plank, season with salt, pepper and butter. Pipe potatoes around the edge of plank and arrange other vegetables attractively. The plank may be placed in hot oven to reheat if necessary.

If potatoes are to be browned they must be brushed with a mixture of egg and milk before returning to the stove to brown.

Place plank on a platter or in holder and serve immediately.

Sometimes the steak is broiled entirely in the broiling pan, placed on a hot buttered plank with vegetables arranged attractively around it.

Broiled chicken, meat loaf or a thick slice of ham may be prepared and served on a plank with vegetables. A plank of vegetables only is very attractive. Cook each vegetable and then arrange on plank.

Stuffed Flank Steak

Pound a large flank steak until it is flat, then make a stuffing of equal parts of sausage meat and bread crumbs, seasoning with minced onion. Roll up, tie into shape, roll so that when served, the steak will be cut across fibers. Sear in hot fat. Cover with stock or water and let simmer 2 hours or longer. Season gravy, pour over meat and serve.

Spanish Steak

1 flank steak	4 tablespoons cooking oil or drippings
1 cup of sliced onions	2 tablespoons butter
1 cup of canned tomatoes	Salt and pepper to taste

Into a fry pan put cooking oil and sear steak well. Remove, season with salt and pepper, roll up and place in a baking pan. Fry onions in the remaining grease in pan until brown. Spread over steak, pour over the cup of tomatoes, add butter, cover and cook in slow oven one hour or longer. Baste steak several times. Make gravy of drippings by adding a little flour to thicken, and a little water. Pour over steak, serve hot. Broiled mushrooms may be added.

Smothered Steak

Select a thick, good cut of round. Wipe, remove rind and cut into sections suitable to serve. Pound with edge of a heavy plate or steak hammer until well beaten. Dip into flour, covering both sides well.

Into a skillet put a small amount of fat; have very hot, put in the pieces of steak and sear both sides well.

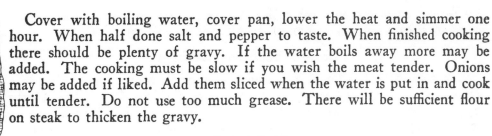

Cover with boiling water, cover pan, lower the heat and simmer one hour. When half done salt and pepper to taste. When finished cooking there should be plenty of gravy. If the water boils away more may be added. The cooking must be slow if you wish the meat tender. Onions may be added if liked. Add them sliced when the water is put in and cook until tender. Do not use too much grease. There will be sufficient flour on steak to thicken the gravy.

Swiss Steak

Select a good round steak, trim and gash edges. Pound with the edge of a thick plate, or steak hammer. Sprinkle well with flour and pound again.

Place on a hot broiling pan, place near the gas blaze and sear, brush over top with butter or drippings, sear again, turn and treat other side same, turn two or three times until as done as liked.

Place on hot platter, salt and pepper, dot with bits of butter, serve at once. This will require about fifteen minutes to cook. If cooked too long it will be tough. Serve with French fried potatoes.

A New Meat Loaf

Prepare the steak the same as for Swiss. Spread the steak with pork sausage half inch thick, season with salt and pepper, roll up the same as making a jelly roll, tie in several places to keep together, place in hot pan and cook in oven 40 to 60 minutes or until the juice is pink, not red. The time depends on the size.

Place on hot platter, remove the strings, serve hot or cold, slicing crosswise. Bread stuffing may be used in place of the sausage. The steak should be an inch thick when using this way.

Meat Loaf

2 lbs. veal or beef ground	1 egg
½ lb. fresh pork ground	½ cup hot water
1 cup bread crumbs	Put butter into hot water, add all
3 tablespoons of butter or substitute	ingredients and mix well
2 teaspoons salt, pepper to taste	

The mixture should be stiff enough to be shaped into a loaf. Place in hot baking pan, sear top quickly, then cook in moderate oven from 30 to 40 minutes, just long enough for the juice to be light pink (test with a fork). If cooked too long it will be dry. Serve hot or cold. Onion or tomato catsup is used in seasoning sometimes.

Mrs. Singer's Beef Jardiniere

2 cups cold roast or soup meat, cut into cubes or strips	1 cup turnips, diced
1 cup celery cut crosswise	1 cup tender snapbeans broken into pieces
1 cup English peas	2 green peppers, shredded
1 cup carrots cut crosswise	

Put into layers in casserole, cover with broth or gravy, season with salt

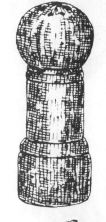

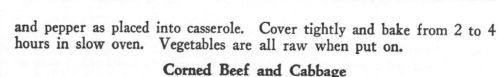

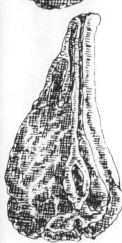

and pepper as placed into casserole. Cover tightly and bake from 2 to 4 hours in slow oven. Vegetables are all raw when put on.

Corned Beef and Cabbage

Soak corned beef 1 hour, drain and cover with cold water; bring to a boil quickly, skim, then simmer for 3 hours or allow 40 minutes to the pound. About three quarters of an hour before serving remove all grease from the liquor. Put a portion of the water from the beef into another kettle, and boil the cabbage until tender, from 30 to 40 minutes.

When cooking just corned beef, 1 carrot, 1 onion and 1 tablespoon vinegar to the pound gives a good flavor.

Allow the meat to remain in the liquor for 30 minutes after the cooking stops.

When ready to serve rub with a bit of butter.

Corned beef sliced and broiled is a good luncheon dish.

Hamburg and Rice Loaf

2 cups hamburg (ground round steak)
½ cup rice
1 cup boiling water
Salt and pepper to taste

4 tablespoons bacon dripping or butter
A few spoonfuls of hot water if too stiff

Wash rice, cook in boiling water until all water is absorbed. Turn into bowl, add meat and seasoning. Add water to make as soft as can handle. Shape into loaf, place in baking pan, cook for forty-five minutes. Serve with hot tomato or creole sauce.

Creole Stew

Put into casserole or Dutch oven a pound of lean meat. Around this put as many potatoes as the family will need, 3 carrots sliced, 1 pint of tomatoes, 1 onion, 1 green pepper with seed removed, 1 cup of butter beans, 3 ears of corn cut from the cob. Sprinkle the top with salt and pepper, fill the vessel with water, put into a slow oven and cook until the meat is tender. Add a little flour thickening, 2 tablespoons of chopped parsley, 2 tablespoons of Worcestershire sauce and one small pod of garlic.

Continue the cooking until seasoning strikes through well. Should the water cook out, replenish when the stew is half done. If added too late it will not be so good.

The gravy is rich and thick, and the entire meal can be cooked with little attention. Serve on a large platter and place the vegetables around the dish.

What is left over can be reheated the next day, and is just as good or better.

Kidney Stew

2 kidneys
1 cup stock
3 tablespoons butter
4 tablespoons flour

1 slice each of onion, carrot, green pepper
1 stalk celery
Salt and pepper to taste

Wash and split kidneys lengthwise, soak in cold water for 2 hours,

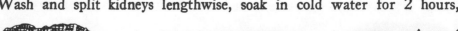

changing water once during the time. Drop into boiling water and cook slowly until tender. When done remove any membrane, cut in thin slices or dice. Make a brown sauce. Slice and cook vegetables in butter; remove; add flour and brown. Add cup of stock, season and add kidneys and let simmer to absorb seasoning.

Serve on toast or in a dish.

Veal Loaf No. 1

2 cups ground veal
1 cup stale bread crumbs
    Enough hot milk to moisten the crumbs

4 tablespoons butter
1 egg
    Season with salt, pepper and parsley

Mix together and bind with well beaten egg. Put into buttered pan, cover with buttered paper and bake in moderate oven about 1 hour. Chicken or rabbit may be used, having the meat raw.

Veal Loaf No. 2

2 lbs. veal from the round
¼ lb. of pork
2 tablespoons tomato catsup
2 tablespoons minced parsley
1 tablespoon grated onion
2 teaspoons salt

1 egg
1 cup dry bread crumbs
3 tablespoons of butter or drippings
    Cayenne pepper to taste (⅛ teaspoon)

After wiping and removing the rind or skin, put the meat through a food chopper. Put all ingredients into meat and mix into a loaf, using a little water if it seems too stiff. Shape into a loaf and bake in moderate oven about 30 minutes, or until it is done. This loaf should be seared on the top to keep in the juices.

Jellied Veal

4 lbs. leg of veal
1 veal knuckle

Salt, pepper and any seasoning wanted

Boil meat until it will fall from bones. Remove bones, shred or grind meat and season. Remove all grease from liquor and reduce to about 3 cups of stock. Put meat into pan, pour over stock just to barely cover the meat. Set aside to jelly. Slice and serve cold or broil.

All seasoning must be added to meat and liquor before putting together. Green and red pepper may be boiled until tender, shredded and mixed with the meat.

To Cook Liver

Have liver cut ¾ inch thick. Pour hot water over it and let stand 15 minutes; take membrane from edge and score well with knife. Salt, pepper and dip in flour, covering well. Into a frying pan put two or three tablespoons of bacon grease and get very hot; sear each piece of liver on both sides, thus browning the flour; when all is browned, cover with boiling

water and cook gently for 15 minutes, or until done as you like. Put on a platter with the gravy; serve very hot. If cooked too long it will be tough. It only takes a few minutes to do the searing.

Beef or calf's liver is good, calf's liver being a little more delicate.

If bacon is to be served with this, first broil the bacon, remove and keep crisp. Use the grease for the liver.

Broiled Liver

Have liver sliced about ½ inch thick. Pour hot water over and let stand 5 minutes, drain, remove the membrane around edge and any other objectionable part.

Into a fry pan place just enough bacon drippings or butter to prevent sticking. Place liver in and turn often, two or three times, until as done as desired.

Place on hot dish, add salt, pepper and melted butter. Serve immediately.

Liver Pudding

Take one hog liver, lights, and one jowl. Boil all together until tender. Mash well or grind in food chopper. Add 1½ or 2 cups of cooked rice, 1 medium size onion chopped fine, salt and pepper to taste. Pack in a bowl.

Philadelphia Scrapple

We use the head and feet of the hog with beef brisket equivalent to half the weight of the pork used. The head and feet well cleaned are put on to boil with the brisket in salted water, which just covers the meat. Boil slowly until the meat leaves the bone and you have a rich stock. When cool enough to handle, grind the meat in a food chopper and strain the stock for bone particles. Add the stock to the ground meat in a heavy vessel and bring to a boil, then add alternately a cup of corn meal and a cup of oatmeal until it is the consistency of mush. Stir continuously for about twenty minutes as it has a tendency to stick. Season with salt and red pepper to taste, add sweet marjoram. About one-third box of sweet marjoram will season about eighteen pounds of pork. Pour into loaf pans and when cold slice and fry in a hot frying pan. Sage may be used in place of the marjoram.

Scrapple

Boil 1 hog liver until tender, take up, mash fine and return to stock, or part of it if there is very much. Add 1 pint sifted meal, salt, pepper and a little sage. Press, slice, cook in oven to brown or broil.

Brains and Eggs

1 set brains	2 tablespoons butter
2 or 3 eggs	Salt and pepper to taste

Soak brains in cold salt water until they will clean easily. Remove all membrane, drop into boiling water and boil until tender, about fifteen

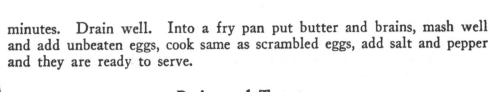
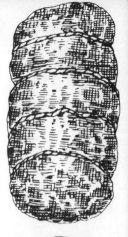

minutes. Drain well. Into a fry pan put butter and brains, mash well and add unbeaten eggs, cook same as scrambled eggs, add salt and pepper and they are ready to serve.

Brains and Tomatoes

2 sets brains (calves brains preferred)	3 tablespoons flour
	1 teaspoon salt
1 pint can tomatoes cooked and strained	1/8 teaspoon cayenne pepper
3 tablespoons butter	1 teaspoon each grated onion, chopped parsley, Worcestershire sauce

Soak brains in cold salt water for one hour, clean, boil until tender, chill. Slice and broil in the butter, remove to platter. To the butter add flour and brown. Add seasoning, cook for one minute, add tomatoes, blend together, cook for ten minutes. Pour over brains as a sauce. Serve on toast. Each slice of brains may be placed on toast and the sauce poured over all. Tomato puree may be used adding equal amount of water. The dish must be hot to be good.

Creamed Sweetbreads

1 lb. sweetbreads	1 teaspoon salt
1 tablespoon chopped parsley	1/8 teaspoon white pepper
1 cup white sauce	

Boil and remove the skins or membrane from the sweetbreads. Make the usual white sauce, add to sweetbreads, add seasoning. Serve in timbales or on toast.

Broiled Sweetbreads

Wash and boil sweetbreads for 30 minutes. Cool, remove any outside membrane, slice lengthwise, sprinkle with salt and pepper. Into a fry pan put a small portion of butter, just sufficient to brown sweetbreads and prevent sticking. Cook for about 5 minutes, browning both sides; place on hot platter, pour over a portion of melted butter and serve at once.

Very small tender sweetbreads may be broiled without boiling, cooking longer to get done. They may be sliced or not. Soak in cold water before broiling. Remove any ends of membrane around edge.

LAMB

Lamb is plain, everyday food, yet it is one which may be dressed up with frills and furbelows if you wish. There are choice, and very choice, cuts—there are plain and very plain parts which anyone may have if they only "know how" to buy.

Anyone should be able to tell lamb from mutton by two distinct ways, the size of a whole lamb weighs about twenty-five to thirty pounds and a quarter is a small portion. The other way, examine the bone where the foot has been removed, the bone is ridged like knuckles, for the foot of a lamb is broken off, not chopped.

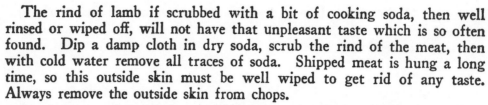

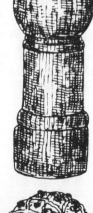

The rind of lamb if scrubbed with a bit of cooking soda, then well rinsed or wiped off, will not have that unpleasant taste which is so often found. Dip a damp cloth in dry soda, scrub the rind of the meat, then with cold water remove all traces of soda. Shipped meat is hung a long time, so this outside skin must be well wiped to get rid of any taste. Always remove the outside skin from chops.

Lamb is roasted, broiled or stewed the same as beef, so if you know how to cook one you know how to cook all.

Many like a boiled leg of lamb, hot or cold. There are many ways of using lamb while we are waiting for fried chicken to come in, so take your choice and see how well the family will like it.

Mutton is the grown lamb. To cook, follow recipes for lamb, cooking a longer period.

Crown Roast of Lamb

A crown roast is a very handsome dish and is made from the loin and rib chops, requiring enough ribs to make the crown. The ribs are separated at the backbone, but left together, so when serving the knife goes down between each rib, through the cut, and the section is lifted out and served. A crown roast is prepared by the butcher. The ribs are frenched and form the crown. A good sized crown will weigh 8 or 10 pounds.

To Cook a Crown Roast

Wipe, salt and pepper the roast. Cover each end of the ribs with a cube of boiling meat or a small Irish potato, or wrap with several thicknesses of wax paper.

Place in hot oven for 15 minutes to sear; reduce heat to 300 F. and add a cup of hot water, to prevent the drippings from scorching, and baste frequently. Cook 1½ hours or longer according to size, the same as roasting. Do not cover, cook in an open pan.

A cup pressed down in center will keep the roast a nice shape. Sometimes a force meat is used as a filling for the center. However, I prefer potatoes or some other vegetable filled in, after roasting.

Roast Leg o' Lamb

Scrub lamb well with soda and wipe the meat off with cold water. Dry. Rub over with some kind of fat and sprinkle with flour. Place in baking pan and sear well on both sides, having a hot oven, or under the flame of a gas range. Reduce heat, add one cup of hot water, roast twenty minutes to the pound, basting occasionally. When half done, salt, pepper and add any seasoning desired, catsup, onion or mustard.

Turn to brown all sides. If water cooks away, add more, a little at a time. Cook in open pan. When done, serve with mint sauce or plain.

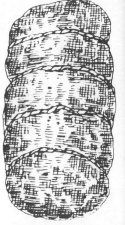

Smothered Lamb

1 small forequarter of lamb	4 tablespoons of bacon drippings or butter
2 carrots	1 tablespoon Worcestershire sauce
2 onions	2 teaspoons salt
1 clove of garlic	Cayenne pepper to taste
1 green pepper	

Boil or steam lamb until very tender, in just enough water to cover.

Into a fry pan put bacon drippings and cut and brown slightly all the vegetables. Place lamb in baking pan, add vegetables and two cups of the water in which it was boiled.

Cook slowly until meat is browned and well seasoned, about one hour. The meat may be sprinkled with flour several times during the cooking. This helps to brown and thicken the sauce or gravy. A cupful of tomatoes, a teaspoon of prepared mustard may be added if liked.

This is good served with macaroni, rice or bread and butter.

To Broil Lamb Chops

Prepare the chops by removing the outside skin and any extra fat. Have a very hot frying pan or skillet, place the chops in it and as soon as the side next to pan is browned, turn. Turn several times, keeping pan hot, never cover, cook about eight to ten minutes. The chops should be about one inch thick. When done remove to a hot platter, season with salt, pepper and melted butter. Serve at once.

Lamb Cutlets

Boil breast of lamb until very tender. When half done, season with salt and pepper and slice of onion. Let stay in water until cold. Cut portions of lamb, roll in beaten egg, then crumbs, fry in deep fat until a nice brown.

Lamb Chops With Eggplant

Have as many chops as guests. Remove the piece of backbone leaving the rib bone, and mash as flat as possible.

Broil nicely and place a chop on a thick slice of fried eggplant. Make a brown sauce of brown butter, flour and stock or milk. Season highly with Worcestershire and chili sauce; pour over all and serve.

Lamb Chops With Grape Jelly

Broil chops—salt, pepper and spread a portion of butter over each chop. Have ½ cup of thin brown sauce ready, add to this ½ glass of grape jelly, blend together well and add a little kitchen bouquet or Worcestershire sauce. Season well with salt and pepper, and pour around the chop. Serve at once.

Lamb Stew

2 pounds of lamb stew	2 sweet green peppers
4 tablespoons of bacon drippings	3 whole cloves
1 large onion	1 can tomatoes, about two cups
1 bunch of carrots (or two cupfuls)	Salt and pepper to taste
1 cup diced celery	

Cut lamb to pieces and sear in the bacon grease. Cut all vegetables in small pieces, add tomatoes, vegetables and seasoning, cook slowly until very tender. Add a little water if necessary.

When done, remove grease if too much, add a little flour or half cup of bread crumbs to thicken, serve over dry rice. Irish potatoes may be boiled, diced and added to take the place of the rice.

Barbecued Lamb

Use any part of the forequarter of lamb. Cook as smothered lamb (see recipe). Add barbecue sauce in place of vegetables, continue cooking until very tender and well seasoned.

PORK

Pork Roast With Dressing

Select pork, have a pocket prepared by the butcher and stuff with the following:

1 cup chopped apples	1 teaspoon salt
2 cups soft bread crumbs	1/8 teaspoon pepper
1 cup of seedless raisins	1 tablespoon butter
1 teaspoon chopped onion	3/4 cup hot water

Mix apples, crumbs, all seasoning and raisins together. Melt butter in hot water, add to other mixtures, use for stuffing.

Goose, duck, birds, veal breast, or spare ribs may be used same as pork.

Roast Pork and Sweet Potatoes

Loin roast or shoulder of ham	Medium size sweet potatoes cut in
Salt	half lengthwise
Pepper	

Season roast with salt and pepper, cook in open pan in moderate oven, 30 to 40 minutes per pound, basting occasionally with the drippings, turning once or more. Boil potatoes until half done, drain and place around roast 45 minutes before serving. Baste potatoes and turn several times to season. Serve potatoes around roast. Gravy may be made from drippings left in roasting pan. For different flavor crush and sprinkle four or five ginger wafers over roast while cooking.

Pork Tenderloin

Slice tenderloin about half inch thick, broil on broiler exactly as steak, giving a little longer time and keep turning. Place on hot platter, season with salt, pepper and butter. Serve with tiny thin hoecakes.

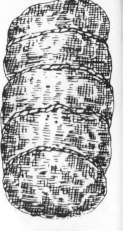
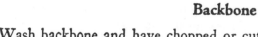

Backbone

Wash backbone and have chopped or cut into pieces convenient to serve. Sprinkle with salt and pepper, place in a baking pan and add two cups of boiling water. Have oven hot for 10 minutes then cook with medium heat. Baste and turn, cook about two hours. If a crusty outside is liked dredge with flour when half done and cook uncovered.

When ready to serve, remove from pan, pour off all grease from top of gravy, add sufficient browned flour to thicken. Serve with baked sweet potatoes.

Boiled Backbone With Macaroni or Dumplings

Prepare bones for cooking, drop into boiling water and boil gently for two or more hours, add salt and pepper when half done. Cook until tender. Have ready some cooked and blanched macaroni, add to backbones and cook just long enough to season well. Dumplings may be used in place of macaroni.

Stuffed Spareribs

Select a long strip of spareribs, wash and dry. Make the usual dressing of stale bread using a portion of corn muffin crumbs. Season with salt, pepper and any other seasoning at hand or liked, such as celery, parsley, onions. Place stuffing on half of the strip, fold over the other half, bringing the sides together forming a pocket. Fasten with stout toothpicks and a string or skewers. Sprinkle with flour, place in baking pan, roast until meat is tender and brown. Use moderate heat for roasting. No water is used, but if ribs seem tough, a very little may be used, allowing it to steam, then dry out and brown.

Spareribs and Sauerkraut

Boil ribs until very tender, having right good quantity of water. Salt to taste. When done, remove ribs and drop in sauerkraut, boil for 20 to 30 minutes, drain and place on platter; arrange ribs around the mound. Serve with some of the raw kraut and baked sweet potatoes.

To Boil a Ham

Scrub a ham until the rind is clean. Soak overnight in cold water if necessary. Put into large boiler and cover with cold water. Let come to the boil slowly and simmer until done, allowing twenty minutes to a pound. Let stay in the water until cold; remove and trim off the skin and any undesirable parts. If very fat, remove a portion. Into the fat and rind rub brown sugar, using about 1 cup, then cover the top with bread crumbs; stick one dozen cloves over the top and dot with spots of black pepper. Dampen the end of finger, dip into the black pepper and press onto the ham; place in oven and brown quickly and it is ready to serve either hot or cold.

To test if done, insert a sharp fork or hat pin in the thickest part on under side. If the juice is pink it is done, if red it is not and must be

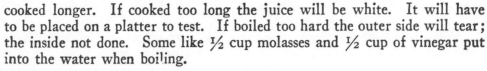

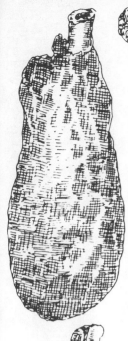

cooked longer. If cooked too long the juice will be white. It will have to be placed on a platter to test. If boiled too hard the outer side will tear; the inside not done. Some like ½ cup molasses and ½ cup of vinegar put into the water when boiling.

To Bake a Ham in Dough

Select a ham which you can depend on as not being too salty. Wash and scrub and soak overnight in cold water if necessary. Remove and wipe dry and let the outer side dry out so it will hold the paste. Mix flour and water to a very stiff paste—almost a dough. Cover the ham well with this (about ¼ inch), and pat dry flour over so you can handle. Place skin side down. Put into a baking pan and place in a hot oven for ten minutes or more until the dough hardens a little; then reduce heat and cook in a slow oven twenty minutes for every pound. When done, test, using a hat pin the same as when boiling. Let get cool; remove the flour well; trim to look nice; rub with brown sugar; cover with bread crumbs, and brown in quick oven. It is then ready to serve hot or cold. Cloves and pepper may be added the same as when boiled. There is no water used at all; the ham is baked in a dry pan.

There is no basting required. If you are sure the ham is sweet, soaking overnight is not necessary.

There is a grade which does not require the soaking. A ham cooked this way is very juicy and most delicious. A half of one could be cooked this way nicely. The cut end would be sealed up.

Baked Ham

Select a ham of dependable make. Scrub and place in a baking pan with a trivet or rack to hold it from resting on the bottom. Put skin side on rack, place in hot oven for fifteen to twenty minutes with fire hot to sear outside, reduce heat to low (275 degrees F.) and bake twenty minutes to the pound. No basting is necessary. Never cover—have open pan. When done let cool sufficiently to handle. Remove skin and trim off any objectional outside. First rub with a bit of mustard, dry or mixed; then rub all over with sugar as much as will soak in. Cover skin side with bread crumbs. Brown in quick oven. If doubtful soak ham in cold water overnight, wipe dry and follow directions. Sweet spiced vinegar is sometimes used with the mustard to give flavor. For very fancy ham, over the crumbs place slices of canned pineapple with a red cherry (maraschino) in the center of each pineapple ring, and brown.

Baked Ham With Red Apples

Arrange slices of hot baked ham on large platter, covering generously with essence of ham. Arrange baked apples around the ham, allowing one apple for each slice of ham. Apples should be hot.

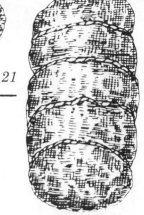

Ham Loaf

1½ cups raw ground ham, fat and lean
1½ cups cold rice
1 cup bread crumbs
1½ cups white sauce
4 stalks celery

1 large onion
2 pimentoes
2 sprigs of parsley
1 teaspoon salt
⅛ teaspoon pepper or more

When ham is ground put seasoning through the food chopper.

Grease and flour a loaf bread pan well, pack meat in pan, place pan into another pan containing hot water, and bake 1 hour.

Serve hot or cold.

Tomato sauce may be used and makes a nice change.

Sugared Ham

1 slice ham, one inch thick
1 cup dark brown sugar, more if needed

4 cloves
½ cup water
Vinegar, water for soaking

Trim ham and place in sufficient tart vinegar and water to cover well. Let soak two hours. Drain and wipe well. Cover with sugar, rub in well, do this on both sides, place into a baking dish, pour over the half-cup water, stick in cloves, cover top with more sugar. Bake slowly for 2 hours. Remove from pan, make sauce of dripping, using flour and water with sauces to season well. Serve the sauce in separate dish. Cider in place of water is more delicious if easy to obtain.

Baked Slice of Ham

Center cut of ham about 3 inches thick
1 cup of boiling water
3 tablespoons vinegar

½ cup brown sugar
Spices (as desired, cloves, cinnamon, etc.)

Place slice of ham in baking pan and pour 1 cup of boiling water with vinegar and half of the brown sugar over it. Bake for two hours in moderate oven—350 degrees. When half done add a sprinkle of spices and remainder of brown sugar, basting occasionally until done. To carve, cut diagonally thru slice beginning at one end. If ham is salty or very dry, it may be soaked several hours in cold water before baking.

Delicious Ham No. 1

Soak a slice of ham in equal parts of sweet milk and water for an hour then wipe and broil as usual.

Delicious Ham No. 2

One slice of ham 1½ inches thick; trim off the skin and rind; sprinkle with brown sugar, using two teaspoons; place in casserole or baking pan; pour over 1½ cups of sweet milk (or just cover); bake in moderate oven one hour. Serve with hominy.

Sizzled Ham

Purchase boiled ham, having it sliced quite thin. In a hot skillet broil until crisp; drain free of any grease; serve with fried hominy (grits).

To Broil Ham

Cut slices of usual thickness. Have heavy skillet hot; trim edges of slices and put into pan; turn several times until done. To make red gravy, sprinkle each good-sized slice with 1 teaspoon of sugar; broil, turning twice until the outer surface is well seared and meat done, remove to platter. Keep the fry pan hot, but not burning. Put in several tablespoons of water to make the gravy, pour over the ham. The sugar caramels and makes the red gravy. An iron skillet makes redder gravy than any other ware. To broil in a gas oven, treat in same way, placing near the flame, turn until done, make gravy in the pan and pour over the meat.

Etowah Ham Loaf

4 cups ground lean ham	3 pimentoes
1 cup finely chopped celery	2 green (bell) peppers
1 cup crushed snowflake crackers	1 small onion
½ cup mayonnaise	1 tablespoon lemon juice
1 box of granulated gelatine dissolved in ½ cup of cold water	3 tablespoons salad dressing
	3 hard boiled eggs

Grind and measure ham. Grind peppers and onion. Chop celery very fine. Dice eggs. Break crackers with fingers (do not roll). Then measure. Melt gelatine over boiling water. Mix all into the ham, add gelatine and mix well. Last, add the mayonnaise and mix well with forks; turn into mold to get firm. This slices nicely and will serve about fifteen. Serve on lettuce with more mayonnaise or as a cold meat.

Ham a la King

2 cups cooked and diced lean ham	2 green peppers, boiled, skinned and cut fine, seed removed
2 cups white sauce	½ cup top milk or thin cream
1 cup chopped mushrooms	4 egg yolks
½ cup chopped almonds (blanched)	Salt and pepper to taste
2 pimentoes, chopped	

Use cold boiled lean ham. Make white sauce; mix all ingredients, using double boiler. Mix yolks of eggs into the milk, add to the mixture and cook until thick.

The cooking of the eggs thickens mixture. Serve in timbales, on toast, or from a serving dish.

Mock Sweetbreads

1 cup of minced lean ham	1½ cups of white sauce
1 cup of diced hard-boiled eggs	Salt and pepper to season

Into a skillet put minced ham and sear until it is partly crisp. Mix all together and fill green, sweet peppers, cover top with buttered crumbs, put

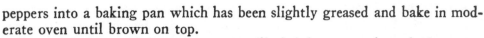

peppers into a baking pan which has been slightly greased and bake in moderate oven until brown on top.

Do not bake too long or peppers will shrink too much to look pretty. Cover bottom of pan with hot water. This will keep the peppers plump. To make in baking dish, slice in rings or grind 2 green peppers to flavor. Cover top with buttered crumbs.

Ham Mousse

2 cups boiled lean ham, ground before measuring
1 cup whipped cream
1 cup cooked mayonnaise
1 tablespoon chili sauce

1 teaspoon prepared mustard
⅛ teaspoon cayenne
2 tablespoons gelatine, dissolved in 1/3 cup cold water

Dissolve gelatine in cold water for five minutes, then melt over boiling water and let cool slightly. Mix with the dressing, add the seasoning, then the whipped cream. Into this mix the ham. Pour into wet mold and let stand until congealed. Serve as a cold meat, in mold or sliced.

Ham Rolls

Cut thin, large slices of baked ham, spread lightly with mayonnaise, then minced cucumber pickles, roll up like a sweet wafer, fasten with a toothpick, stick an olive on the end of the pick, place on platter, garnish with parsley and olives, or roll each ham roll in wax paper, twist each end and it is ready to serve at the picnic. Boiled ham may be used just as well.

FOWL

To Dress a Turkey

The turkey is better to bleed when killed, as it gives whiter meat and the feathers are usually dry picked. Hold turkey over a gas flame or burning paper to singe off the long hair-like feathers. Turn every side, open wings so all parts may be reached.

Place in pan of water, scrub skin well, rinse and dry. Remove feet at first joint. The sinews may be pulled out with the removal of feet, but it is much easier to remove them after cooking. Place turkey on table, and with a large knife or cleaver chop off head, leaving a long neck. Push back the skin and remove neck near the shoulders, leaving the skin intact. Make a long cut at back of neck through the skin and remove crop. This leaves the breast covered with skin.

Turn turkey on its back, make a generous cut (about 2 inches) crosswise at the end of the breast bone; make the second cut just through the skin near the end of fowl, leaving a wide section of skin. Free skin under the "parson's nose"; this frees the intestines. Pull out through the opening at the end of the breast bone, drop for a moment, insert the fingers and free the gizzard and other organs joining the backbone. Remove carefully without breaking. Examine to see that every part has been removed —heart and lungs. Remove oil sac. Rinse well with cold water and dry.

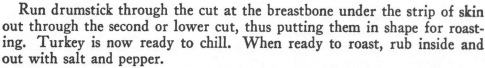

Run drumstick through the cut at the breastbone under the strip of skin out through the second or lower cut, thus putting them in shape for roasting. Turkey is now ready to chill. When ready to roast, rub inside and out with salt and pepper.

When stuffing: Fill opening where crop was removed, being careful not to crowd, leaving room for swelling. Sew up cut at the back, in the skin which covered the neck, draw skin together at neck bone, leaving it loose. Gather and tie with string; this gives a beautiful, round, full breast. Skin of neck is tucked under back until roasted. Fill carcass with stuffing, not crowding, truss wings by using a coarse needle and thread—one stitch in each wing, turning to hold flat to the body. The strings in all three places should be removed before sending to the table.

To Dress a Hen

Use directions for turkey. Hens are picked dry, or scalded.

To Roast a Turkey

After the stuffing is made and put in the turkey, make a thin paste of melted butter and flour and rub over turkey. Place in baking pan with a trivet or something to lift bird slightly from the pan. Place in hot oven to sear the outside until it just begins to brown; if kept too long the skin might burst. When seared, lower the heat, toss over the turkey a cup of hot water and melted butter.

Now the real roasting beings. Never cover, leave open, basting often with the drippings in the pan. Should the water cook away, add half a cup more, just enough to prevent drippings from scorching. Turn turkey to brown on all sides. Allow 25 minutes to a pound and cook slowly (about 275 degrees) until done and well browned. The last half hour turn breast down so the juices will flow to the white meat.

If turkey is very large and any part should be sufficiently brown, cover with a greased cloth or paper of several thicknesses to prevent burning.

A turkey cooked in an open pan is far better and just as tender as when cooked in a roaster.

The giblets, neck, gizzard and liver are boiled in water to make the gravy. Use stock and minced giblets with drippings in the roasting pan.

Never parboil a turkey, it loses its sweetness. To test when done, pull the wing or thigh bone loose from the body. If it breaks easily and the joint shows no red meat, it is done. Never stick a fork in a turkey or choice roast, as it allows the juice to escape. Some turkeys cook much quicker than others, due to the condition of the fowl. A very large turkey will require slower cooking than one weighing 10 or 12 pounds.

Creamed Turkey

See recipe for Creamed Chicken.

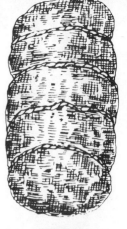

To Broil Chickens

Use young chickens weighing from a half to three-fourths pounds each. Dress and cut in half. Bend drumstick back to thigh, and cut through the muscle to make joint limp, shape and place in pan, skin side up. Broil, adding small amount of butter, turning often to prevent burning. Season while cooking. When done, remove to platter, make gravy of the browned juices and butter, and pour over the chicken.

Toast may be arranged around the platter, or each half of chicken placed on a piece.

Very young chickens are not fat, so require quite a bit of butter.

To Smother Broil Chickens

Prepare young chickens the same as for broiling. Place in hot broiling pan, skin side down; dot with butter and place under blaze in broiling oven. Cook until seared, turn, dot with butter and broil again, keeping pan far enough from the blaze to prevent butter catching fire. When both sides are browned, add a cup of hot water (the amount depending on the number of chickens being broiled) and let steam and cook in pan; add seasoning and plenty of butter; let cook slowly until very tender, turning and browning. More water may be required. When tender, allow all liquid to cook away and again crisp the chicken. There should be sufficient butter to do this. Place on platter, make brown gravy, pour over the chickens and serve.

A few spoons of water added to the hot pan will make gravy of the browned juices and butter. Garnish with parsley, broiled pineapple, peaches or tomatoes. Mushrooms may be added during the cooking if used. A cream or thick gravy is sometimes preferred.

To Pan Smother Broil Chicken

Prepare chicken and broil as directed for broiling. After searing on both sides several times, add a few spoons of water, cover to steam to make very tender, repeating if necessary. When tender, remove top, broil down until chicken is crisp and serve immediately.

Make gravy by adding a little water to the juice and butter. Salt and pepper during the cooking. This way of cooking makes the chicken very tender.

Chicken and Ham a la Georgia
(A Company Dish)

Broil small chickens as usual, having ½ chicken for each guest. Place chicken in center of large platter. Arrange slices of hot baked ham around chicken. Over each slice of ham put a generous spoon of the ham essence. This blends with the chicken gravy and is most delicious. Serve chicken, ham and gravy to each guest.

To Clean and Dress Chicken for Frying

Remove feathers, wash with a coarse cloth, singe to remove pin feathers

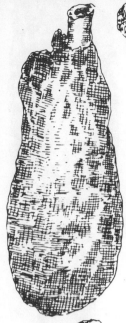
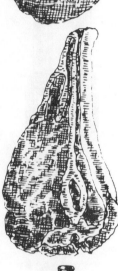

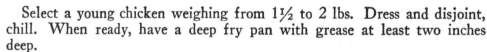

and wash again. Remove drumstick and second joint together, then wings, crop and oil bag. Slip knife under the shoulder blade, which runs parallel with the backbone; cut towards the breast to free the bone. With the left hand, catch the shoulder blades near the breast, take neck and backbone with the right hand and tear the two pieces apart, thus freeing the entrails. Remove the gizzard and liver. Cut breast in half lengthwise and disjoint the drumstick. Cut the back in two pieces; this gives 6 meaty pieces and 6 bony pieces. Rinse and chill. Some like to salt chicken when setting aside to chill. Care must be taken not to break or cut too near the gall bag. Cut through the thick side of the gizzard down to the lining which holds the grit; peel off the outside and rinse until it is clear.

All fowl should be chilled thoroughly to remove the body heat.

Fried Chicken

Select a young chicken weighing from 1½ to 2 lbs. Dress and disjoint, chill. When ready, have a deep fry pan with grease at least two inches deep.

Sift enough flour in which to roll the chicken pieces (a cup and a half or two cups). Add salt and pepper to the flour, roll each piece in flour and place in the hot grease. Put the largest pieces in first and on the hottest part of the pan. When all is in, cover for 5 minutes. Remove top and turn when the underside is well browned. Replace top for another 5 minutes, remove and cook in open pan until the bottom side is browned. About 30 minutes in all will be required for cooking chicken if it is not too large. Do not turn chicken but once; too much turning and too long cooking will destroy the fine flavor which is there when well cooked.

The fat should be deep enough to cover the pieces when it boils up.

To make cream gravy:

Pour off the grease, leaving 2 to 3 tablespoons in the pan with the browned crumbs. Add 2 tablespoons butter, 4 tablespoons flour, blend and cook until a golden brown; add 1 cup milk and 1 cup hot water. Stir until smooth and the right thickness and add salt and black pepper. Pour into a gravy boat and serve with hot biscuit or dry rice. Never pour gravy over chicken if you wish Georgia fried chicken.

Baked Chicken

Select a nice, plump hen in good condition. Prepare for cooking. Make a stuffing and fill chicken after it has been salted and peppered. Rub over the outside with butter and sprinkle with flour. Place in a roaster and put in hot oven to sear. When seared well, cover and reduce heat to medium or slow. Roast until done. Remove top and brown again to make crisp.

Make gravy of drippings in the pan, and giblets; thicken with flour. About 2 cups of water, milk or stock will be needed for the gravy, and 2 tablespoons flour for thickening. If flour is browned more will be required than when white is used.

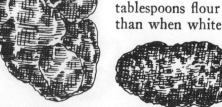

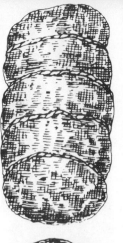

Roasted Capon

Prepare and roast exactly the same as turkey. Capon will cook very easily. Stuff the same as turkey and make gravy with giblets.

Chicken Surprise

1 cooked hen	2 teaspoons salt
1 tablespoon butter	¼ teaspoon pepper
1 cup sweet milk	

Put hen through meat chopper and mix with other ingredients; roll out small pieces of biscuit dough, little larger than a tea cup; put in a spoonful of the meat, wet edges, draw up, make a ball; fry a nice brown in deep fat.
This will make about 2 dozen.
Use a frying basket.
It is better to have meat warm.
Cook and serve immediately.
Use more or less milk to moisten the meat.

Dish for Sunday Night Supper

Take breast of cold chicken or any meaty pieces and with scissors cut into pieces like fingers. Have a dish of cooked cauliflower flowerettes about the size of half a dollar.

Place leaves of lettuce on platter; on each leaf put slice of tomato and on this a piece of chicken, strips of pimento, a spoonful of mayonnaise and on this the cauliflower. To be passed. Any combination desired may be used.

Chicken Gumbo

1 young hen	3 tablespoons of butter if the chicken
1 quart okra	is not very fat (or bacon drip-
6 ripe tomatoes	pings).
1 large onion	Salt and pepper to taste

Boil the chicken until very tender. Pull the meat from the bones and return to the water in which it was cooked—there should be about three cups of water.

Peel and chop the tomatoes; cut okra in small pieces, also the onion; add seasoning and cook slowly until the vegetables are done and the mixture is thick; stir often as you would a hash or Brunswick stew. Sometimes chicken and rice are cooked together this way. The latter dish I call "pilau."

Chicken Brunswick Stew

1 fowl	1 pint of butterbeans
1 quart of corn	2 onions
1 quart of tomatoes	Salt and pepper to taste
1 pint of okra	

Boil chicken until it will leave the bones and be very tender. Pull meat from bones and cut into large cubes, return to the water in which it was

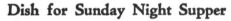
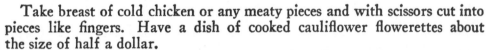

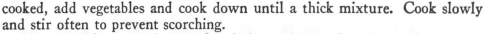

cooked, add vegetables and cook down until a thick mixture. Cook slowly and stir often to prevent scorching.

All vegetables must be cut fine before adding. Bread crumbs may be added to thicken chicken if necessary; use only the crumbs.

Creamed Chicken

One hen boiled until tender, remove meat from bones, cut in cubes as for salad. Make the usual white sauce and mix with the chicken, usually two cups of chicken will require one or one and a half of white sauce. Season with salt and pepper to taste. Use white or red pepper. Use about four tablespoons of flour for one cup of milk in making the white sauce. Canned mushrooms (or fresh ones) are often put with creamed chicken, as well as celery and pimentoes. The celery is cut small, boiled until tender, drained and added.

Chicken a la King

1 hen	1 cup chopped almonds (blanched)
1 can mushrooms	Yolks of 4 eggs
3 green peppers	2 cups of white sauce
2 pimentoes	Salt and cayenne pepper to taste
½ cup cream	

Boil hen until tender, as for salad; dice, remove all skin and veins. Make white sauce the usual way. Remove seed from green peppers, boil until tender in salt water; remove the skin and chop with red peppers, blanch and chop almonds. Put all the ingredients into the white sauce while it is hot (in a double boiler); beat yolks of eggs into cream; add to mixture and cook over hot water until the eggs are cooked and it thickens. Serve in timbales, on toast, or from a serving dish. This will serve about one dozen.

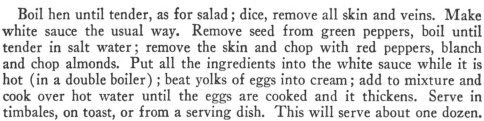

Chicken Shortbread

Make the usual egg bread and bake as directed. (See recipe for Egg Bread.) Cut in pieces about 4 inches square. Split open. Have ready creamed chicken, place bottom piece of bread on plate, cover top with creamed chicken, place top piece of bread and cover generously with more creamed chicken. Garnish with minced parsley and serve piping hot. Chicken a la King may be used. Served with a drink this as a meal within itself.

Chicken Croquettes

Boil a chicken (hen) until very tender, pick meat from bones, rejecting any gristle and skin. Put through food chopper.

For every cup of ground chicken use half a cup of white sauce, season with salt, pepper and finely chopped parsley. Mix and set aside to get cold so the croquettes may be shaped; then make into any desired shape, roll in fine, dry bread crumbs, beaten egg, then crumbs again. Fry in deep fat until a golden brown. Drain on paper napkin. Use the whole egg, add one tablespoon of cold water to the egg.

Have the mixture soft so the inside will be soft and creamy. Do not put

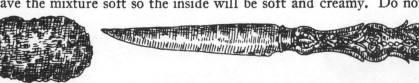

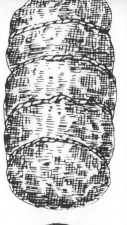

raw eggs into croquettes, it makes them tough. One hen usually makes about two dozen croquettes.

Molded Chicken

2 cups chicken broth
4 egg yolks
2 tablespoons flour
2 tablespoons gelatine soaked in 1/3 cup of water or stock

2 cups finely chopped chicken
2 cups whipped cream
Salt and pepper to taste

Put gelatine to soak for five minutes, mix flour to smooth paste with a small quantity of broth, add balance of broth which has been heated. Cook until thick, add gelatine and thoroughly melt, add chicken and seasoning. Let get cold. Add whipped cream, turn into mold to get firm, small or large, serve on lettuce with mayonnaise.

Hot Chicken Mold

2 cups cooked ground chicken
1 cup thin white sauce

3 eggs
Season with salt and pepper

Boil chicken until very tender, remove from bones and put through food chopper. Mix with the white sauce, season, add eggs which have been beaten together, mix well and pour into a buttered mold. Steam about 30 to 40 minutes or until done in moderate oven. Unmold on a platter, pour over all a brown nut sauce, serve very hot. This is for a meat or an entree.

Chicken Mousse No. 1

1 cup cooked chicken put through food chopper
3 tablespoons cold white sauce

1 tablespoon spiced vinegar
Whites 2 eggs
Salt and pepper to suit taste

Mix chicken and white sauce; season well with salt and pepper and 1 tablespoon spiced vinegar.

Beat whites of eggs stiff and fold into mixture. Place pan, uncovered, in hot water and cook like cup custard in moderate oven for 15 minutes. Unmold and serve hot with hot white sauce. Individual molds may be used. Have mold well greased.

Chicken Mousse No. 2

1 cup cold cooked chicken put through food chopper (breast preferred)
1/4 lb. fresh mushrooms broiled and put through food chopper

1 tablespoon gelatine dissolved in 1/4 cup chicken broth
1 cup hot chicken broth
Season with salt and pepper very highly

Mix well and set aside to cool. When this begins to stiffen, beat 1 cup of cream stiff and fold into mixture. Pour into mold or form to get firm. Slice and serve on lettuce leaf as a salad or as a cold meat.

Southern Dry Stuffing
(Using Bread Crumbs and Egg Bread)

Make a rich egg bread or corn meal muffins doubling the number of eggs used. Make the day before using for stuffing. Crumble crust and all

using equal amount of dry bread crumbs and egg bread crumbs. Mix same as when using only bread crumbs. Add teaspoon baking powder when mixing. No raw eggs are used. It will require four or five cups each of the dry bread crumbs and egg bread crumbs to fill a 12 pound turkey.

Turkey Stuffing

½ cup butter
4 cups wet bread

Onion, celery, parsley, salt and pepper

Melt butter in skillet, fry the onion and celery to get flavor, then remove. Put the wet bread into the pan, mix well, add salt and pepper and chopped parsley. Fill turkey. Use stale bread, cover with cold water until moist, squeeze dry and use. Use no eggs. This stuffing may be used for hens, fish or any meats.

Dry Stuffing for Turkey or Chicken

4 cups stale dry bread crumbs
¼ lb. butter
1 small onion sliced

2 stalks celery cut very fine
Pepper to taste

Melt butter, cook onion in butter until a golden brown. Remove onion, pour butter over bread crumbs, add celery, pepper and more salt if necessary. Fill turkey or hen with stuffing and roast as directed.

More butter may be used.

Egg bread crumbs may be mixed with the bread crumbs.

Mushrooms or boiled chestnuts may be added to stuffing.

Mushroom Stuffing

Peel and wash fresh mushrooms. Broil in butter and make gravy by adding a little water, chop and add to stuffing, being careful not to lose a drop of the gravy. Add to any one of the recipes for stuffing.

A small quantity of mushrooms (about ¼ lb.) will season, more will be better. Canned mushrooms may be used, but they do not have the same flavor.

Mushroom Stuffing for Turkey

One-half pound fresh mushrooms broiled, then stewed in 2 cups water for 15 minutes. Cut stale bread in slices, then in cubes, fry brown in half cup butter. Mix mushrooms and bread together, being careful not to break the cubes of bread. Fill turkey and roast as usual.

Chestnut Stuffing

For stuffing with chestnuts, make the usual dressing. I prefer the dry crumbs with seasoning and moistened with butter. Peel chestnuts and remove dark skin, boil in salt water until done, which will not require very long. Drain and add to dressing. Use whole or mash. Stuff turkey and roast as usual.

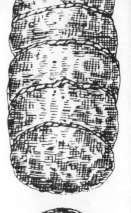

Corn Meal Stuffing

Make a rich egg bread (see recipe for Egg Bread), using more eggs. Let cool, crumble and pulverize crust well. Add melted butter, season with anything desired (see Turkey Stuffing). Fill hen or turkey and roast.

Raisin Stuffing for Poultry

1 cup chopped apples
2 cups soft bread crumbs
1 teaspoon chopped onions
1 teaspoon salt
1/8 teaspoon pepper

1/2 teaspoon poultry seasoning
1 cup seedless raisins
2 tablespoons butter
3/4 cup hot water

Mix apples, crumbs, onion, salt, salt, pepper, poultry seasoning and raisins. Melt butter in hot water and add. Mix thoroughly and use for stuffing goose, duck, turkey, chicken or roast of pork, or birds.

Drop Dumplings

2 cups flour
4 teaspoons baking powder

1 teaspoon salt

Sift together and mix into a dough, using a cup of milk, more or less, as necessary. With a fork and spoon drop into a stew, meat or vegetable, pieces about as large as a walnut. Let boil rapidly 10 minutes, taking care not to uncover pot until dumplings are to be removed. Keeping pot covered causes them to be light and fluffy.

SUGGESTIONS FOR COOKING GAME

The game laws of Georgia for some years have been such that unless you did the hunting, or owned a lodge or plantation, there was no game in store for you, for the choice game is not for sale at the present time.

Our common game are ducks, birds and rabbits, and they're plentiful in many sections, while venison and wild turkey are only for the favored few.

The venison, cooked according to the following instructions, is delicious. For the roast, soak in salt water for six hours, using one tablespoon of salt to enough water to cover. Dry, rub with butter, season with salt and pepper, place in roasting pan, add a sliced onion and one carrot. Place in a hot oven, add a little hot water and roast rapidly, basting frequently with the gravy. Five pounds will require 45 minutes of cooking. Kitchen bouquet, A-1 sauce or any sauces may be added to the gravy. Make gravy as any other gravy and add to it a glass of tart jelly. Keep everything piping hot. The roast may be cooked longer if a very done meat is preferred.

Venison steak should be broiled quickly in a piping hot pan or under a very hot fire. Do not have steak more than half or three-quarters of an inch thick. Turn often and cook 5 to 7 minutes. Place on hot platter and serve very hot.

Wild turkey is prepared and roasted exactly as our domestic ones, perhaps in a little less time. Give it plenty of time, however, for there is noth-

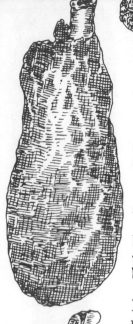

ing quite so bad as a tough turkey. Stuffing or dry rice, with rich brown gravy, cranberries or tart jelly with celery would complete the meal for many.

Vegetables may be added.

Ducks and wild turkeys are stronger than our chickens and turkeys, and some like this, while others dislike the wild flavor.

Ducks usually weigh from three to six pounds. The young fowls may be identified by the wind pipe which is easily broken when pressed between the fingers. The breastbone is soft and almost transparent, and the under-bill will break easily.

A duck is prepared differently from chickens owing to the short legs. Draw the thighs close to the body and hold them by inserting a skewer under the middle joint through the body and under the joint on the other side, wind a string around each end of the skewer, first one side, then the other, to hold the thighs in place and close to the body. Do the wings the same way, running the skewer through wings and body.

Draw the neck skin under the back and secure with a third skewer. Season with salt and pepper, rub inside with one tablespoon of ground ginger and sprinkle with flour. Inside, place a small onion, a medium apple, and the duck is ready to go in the roaster. Ducks are usually quite fat, so a trivet in the roaster or pan is best to hold it up out of the grease.

Ducks, like our turkey, should be carefully prepared and roasted if you want them good. They may be stuffed or not, just as one wishes. Some use the same stuffing as for turkey, and some like a mashed Irish potato stuffing, highly seasoned with onions, tomato catsup, salt and pepper. Usually no stuffing is used, rice being served in place of stuffing. Brown rice and wild rice are particularly good with any kind of game.

It is generally believed that a covered roaster is preferable to an open pan for ducks. Allow 20 minutes per pound. Roast in a very hot oven for the first half hour. Reduce heat slightly for the next half hour and continue the roasting with a fairly hot oven, about 400 degrees. The apple and onion are removed before sending to the table, and so are the skewers and strings. Pour off fat from the roasting pan, leaving only a few spoonfuls to blend with the flour, making the gravy same as for turkey or chicken, using the minced giblets.

A glass of very tart jelly with a little mustard is often added to the gravy, using sufficient water to the flour and grease to make the required amount.

Birds may be broiled, fried or roasted. Broiling is the most popular way. My experience has been that the broiling must be done quickly, not over 10 or 15 minutes if you want them tender and juicy. Use a heavy iron fry pan, slightly greased.

Place the inside of bird next to the pan first. It is necessary to press the bird flat to prevent the legs from sticking up, thus ruining its looks when served.

To keep the legs from sticking up use a flat top slightly smaller than the skillet and a weight. I use an old flat iron as a weight and press down until the bird has gotten hot enough to hold the right shape. Leave space so the steam can escape, and the broiling begins. Turn and broil other side,

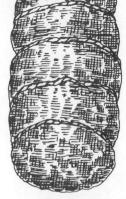

keeping weight on for a moment, then remove top and weight and continue cooking for the given time. Have melted butter ready, salt and pepper when half done. Place on hot platter and serve very hot. Sometimes just the breast is broiled and put on heart-shaped toast. The breast resembles a heart very much and this is quite a pretty way to serve it. The joints may later be used in a pie.

Roast Goose

Select a plump bird, pick and remove the pin feathers. Singe and draw, then wash well in warm water, using a vegetable brush to scrub the skin. Plunge into cold water until chilled. Now place the goose in a preserving kettle and add 1 fagot of soup herbs, and 2 onions. Sufficient boiling water to cover. Bring to a boil and cook for three-quarters of an hour. Remove and let cool. Place ½ cup of shortening in a large frying pan and add 1½ cups of finely chopped onions. Cook until soft and add 2 cups mashed potatoes, 1 cup fine bread crumbs, ½ cup finely chopped parsley, ½ cup finely chopped celery leaves, ½ cup finely chopped pimentos, the meat picked from the neck and giblets, chopped fine, also 1 teaspoon thyme, ¾ teaspoon sweet marjoram, ¼ teaspoon sage, ½ teaspoon poultry seasoning. Cook slowly, turning frequently for one-half hour. Cool and then fill the goose. Sew the opening with darning needle and stout string. Fasten the flap and neck, then rub the bird well with plenty of shortening. Dust thickly with flour. Place in a roasting pan in hot oven for 20 minutes, then commence to baste, using boiling water. Reduce the heat to moderate, turn the goose breast down and cook for two and one-half hours. About one-half hour before removing from the oven turn the bird on its back and let the breast brown nicely. Lift to a warm plate and garnish with baked apples. To make the gravy, drain nearly all the fat from the pan, add sufficient boiling water and cook for a few minutes.

To Roast a Duck

Prepare duck as any fowl; rub with salt and pepper. Take two tablespoons of ground ginger and rub inside and out. Place on inside one small onion which has been cut across the top; into this stick four cloves. Melt ½ cup of butter, add 1 cup hot water, pour over duck and roast, basting often. When nearly done sprinkle with flour and baste often with the gravy. If more water is needed, add. Never have a great quantity at one time.

Ducks are not usually stuffed, but if so desired use a dressing the same as for turkey. Chestnuts may be added and are delicious. Mushrooms, fresh or canned, may be used. The gravy should be highly seasoned.

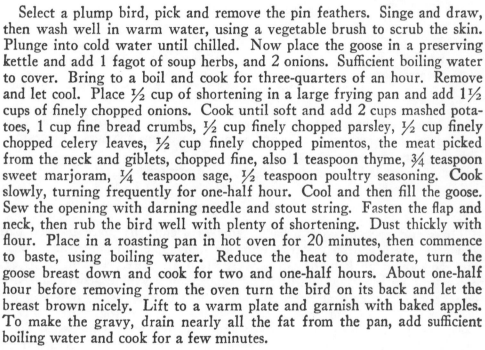

Oftentimes a portion of tart jelly is added to the gravy the last part of the cooking.

Duck Salad

Cut the meat of a cold duck into cubes and season well with a French dressing. Let stand an hour. Drain well and mix with equal quantity of minced celery. Serve with portion of mayonnaise and garnish with slices of orange with the peeling left on.

Diced artichokes will take the place of celery. Scrape and dice small. Dill pickles may be used.

Yorkshire Ducks

½ lb. lean pork
½ lb. beef suet
1 egg
½ lb. veal

1 cup soft bread crumbs
¼ cup water
Season with salt, pepper and sage

Grind meat and suet. Mix bread crumbs and egg with water then blend into the meat; mix well and shape into 6 small loaves. Place in a dripping pan and bake 45 minutes.

Fat pork instead of suet may be used if preferred.

To Cook Squabs

Dress and open down the back, same as a chicken; place in deep pan and cover with boiling water, adding enough apple vinegar to make real tart, boil about an hour or till tender, drain off water, (saving 2 cups), dot squabs with butter, add salt and pepper and sprinkle generously with flour, put in broiler near fire and brown on both sides well; now add the broth, put in oven and cook another hour slowly, adding more water if necessary, letting the gravy be dark and rich, having 2 cups when done. Put on hot platter and pour gravy over. Serve with dry rice. Mushrooms may be added the last hour, which makes a nice dish.

Broiled Birds

Dress birds, open down the back. Flatten open with hands or some heavy implement. Have skillet hot and just slightly buttered to prevent birds sticking. Salt, pepper, place bird in, inside down. With a small top and heavy weight (a sad iron), press on bird to hold flat and keep so, this requires just long enough to get it heated and "set." Turn and repeat until well seared. Turn often to prevent burning. There must be sufficient opening around the edge of pan and top to allow the steam to escape.

After the searing is done the weight is removed, a bit of butter is added. Continue cooking and turning for 8 to 15 minutes. Place on hot dish, dot with butter or use melted. Into the skillet put a tiny bit of hot water to get up all of the browned juices, pour this gravy over the bird, garnish and serve.

Points of toast may be used.

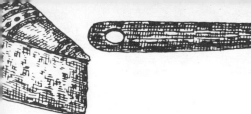

CHAPTER II

Eggs, Omelets, Souffles and Cheese Dishes

Scrambled Eggs a la Stanley

Into a heavy skillet put butter or bacon drippings (1 teaspoon for each egg.) Have pan moderately hot. Break egg in dish and turn into pan. Just as soon as the white begins to cook (turn white) stir gently, allowing more white to reach the pan taking care not to break the yolks until half of the white is cooked; then gently stir white and yolk—continue until cooked sufficiently. By using gentle heat the eggs will be tender and soft but done and most delicious. Serve eggs on a warm dish.

Hard-Boiled Eggs

Drop eggs into warm water, let come to a boil, and continue boiling for 20 minutes. Stir several times at first to prevent yolk from dropping to one side, which would give a very thin white on one side. When done drop into cold water. Crack each shell so water will enter and make the shell come off easily without breaking the white. An egg a day or two old will peel better than a very fresh one.

Soft-Boiled Eggs

Drop egg into boiling water, boil 2 or 3 minutes until cooked as desired.

To Cook an Egg for an Invalid

Take a small saucepan as deep as a tea cup; half fill with boiling water. Into this put a tea cup to get hot. When hot put a small piece of butter and break in the egg. Keep the water boiling and when the white begins to cook, stir from the side of the cup for more to cook; when the white is nearly all a white jelly, break the yolk and continue stirring gently until as stiff as desired; season and serve in the cup in which it is cooked. This is easily done and is good, the egg being very tender and jelly-like.

To Soft Boil an Egg for an Invalid

Fill a quart cup with boiling water to heat, empty and refill; place on table and drop in an egg, cover top with saucer and let the egg stay in for eight minutes. Take out and you have one with a jelly-like white which is very easily digested.

Eggs Poached in Water

Grease a skillet or fry pan and fill with water sufficient to cover eggs. Let water come to the boiling point (but not boil), break and turn each egg into water. Keep water hot, just simmering, until white is cooked and yolk as done as desired. Remove with a perforated spoon and place on toast or platter.

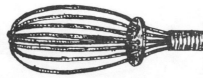

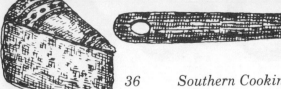

Eggs Cooked in Poacher

Have poacher filled with hot water, and egg container greased. Place an egg in each cup, lower container into hot water and cook until done. Lift out and slide eggs on platter.

Some egg poachers have cups for eggs, and they are cooked entirely by steam from the boiling water below. For this utensil each cup should have a small portion of melted butter ready when eggs are dropped in. Steam until eggs are as firm as desired.

Poached Eggs a la Lewis

(Sunday Night Dish)

Poach as many eggs as needed. Drain and place on a platter.

Make a thick white sauce, season with salt and pepper. Pour over eggs. Place in hot oven to brown slightly on top. Sprinkle top generously with minced parsley and paprika. Serve at once.

In a gas oven place platter under the fire to brown on top.

To Cook Egg Yolks

(1 dozen yolks)

In a saucepan put one quart of hot water, add two teaspoons of salt. Have boiling. With a whip or electric beater whip the yolks until light and frothy. Pour into the water, which should be boiling hard, stirring with egg whip constantly for two or three minutes until small particles show or the mixture has a curdled look. Have ready a strainer lined with 2 layers of cheese cloth. Pour in hot mixture and drain off water. There will be a light, fluffy mixture. Turn on platter and serve as an omelet or to garnish spinach or use as a sandwich base or salad. Grated or cream cheese or mayonnaise may be mixed with the cooked eggs. This is delicious and very versatile.

Another Way to Cook Egg Yolks

Have a sauce pan with sufficient hot water to float the yolks. As the eggs are broken and white removed drop each yolk into the water. When all are in, place pan over a medium heat and boil gently until yolks are firm. Remove and use as any egg yolk for salad, garnishing or sandwiches.

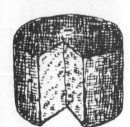

Stuffed Eggs

6 hard boiled eggs	1 tablespoon of prepared mustard
3 slices of crisp broiled bacon	Salt, pepper, bacon drippings or
3 cucumber pickles	butter to season

Place eggs in warm water to boil, shake pan several times to turn the eggs so they will boil more perfectly. Cook about 20 minutes. Crack shells and drop into cold water. Peel and cut in half and remove yolks. With a fork mash yolks to a paste, chop all ingredients into smallpieces and mix with the seasoning into the yolks until well blended.

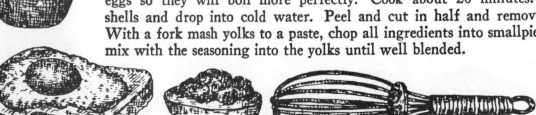

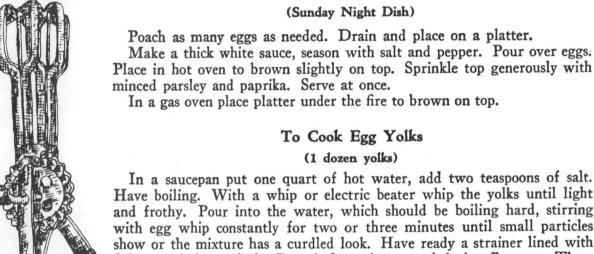

Refill the white sections, having them very full. Arrange daintily on platter, garnish with rings of green pepper and sprigs of parsley.

Baked Eggs

6 eggs   Salt and pepper to taste
⅛ lb. butter

Break eggs into muffin pans, which should be cold, with plenty of fat to prevent sticking, put butter, salt and pepper over each egg. Bake in a moderate oven to suit taste, remove with knife and serve while hot on toast.

Eggs a la Henrietta

6 pieces of buttered toast   ⅛ teaspoon salt for whites of eggs
6 eggs   Salt, pepper and minced parsley

Make toast. Have a pan of very hot water sufficient to float yolks. Separate eggs, dropping yolks in water, and whites in a bowl. Add salt to whites and beat until stiff. Place toast on baking sheet, and on each piece of toast, form a nest of whites, making a depression in the center for the yolks; drop in yolks and place sheet in moderate oven and bake until whites are a delicate brown, and yolks are cooked. Sprinkle with salt, pepper and minced parsley, and serve immediately. The yolks must be lifted from hot water with a slit spoon to drain. The hot water warms and partly cooks yolks and allows them to be handled without breaking.

Puffy Omelet

3 eggs   ½ teaspoon salt
3 tablespoons of water (or sweet-   1 tablespoon butter
    milk)   Dash of cayenne pepper

Use a heavy frying pan or omelet pan; put over a slow fire to heat; gently melt butter, but don't burn; separate egg; beat yolks light, and add water, salt and pepper. Beat whites until quite stiff and firm. Pour the yolk mixture over whites and fold together. Increase heat under pan, and pour the mixture in. Put over medium heat and cover. When risen and brown around the edge, put into a hot oven and finish cooking, and brown top.

When well browned, make a deep cut through the center; fold together and turn out onto a platter. Serve at once. Grated ham, cheese, marmalade, or jelly may be spread on top before folding, if liked.

Spanish Omelet

First Part

3 eggs   2 tablespoons of water
3 tablespoons of butter or oil   Salt and pepper to taste

Put butter into heavy fry pan, beat eggs together until light; add water, turn into hot pan, cover bottom, remove to gentle heat and cook slowly until set.

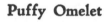

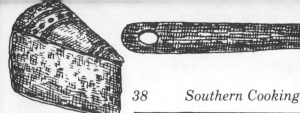

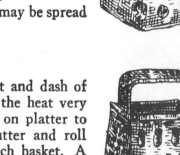

Spread on sauce, roll up, turn onto hot platter and serve at once.

Second Part—Sauce

2 medium tomatoes	2 tablespoons green peas
1 onion	1 pimento
6 large stuffed olives	1 green pepper, which has been par-
2 tablespoons butter	boiled

Peel, chop and drain tomatoes, put butter into pan, grate and add onion and tomatoes; cook for few minutes, add other ingredients; cook gently until ready to pour on omelet. The sauce should be rather dry.

A fluffy omelet is used same way.

Quick Omelet

Break as many eggs as needed into a dish, beat very little, until the yolks and whites are slightly mixed. Into a fry pan put a little butter to melt (about 2 tablespoons for 4 eggs). Pour in the eggs, let cook through until the top is soft, and the part next to the pan slightly browned. Do not turn. Roll up and place on a warm platter. Serve at once.

Any filling—minced bacon, diced ham, creole sauce or jelly may be spread on before rolling and serving.

Traveler's Omelet

Beat 2 eggs together until very light, add ¼ teaspoon salt and dash of pepper. Cook on griddle as you would batter cakes, having the heat very moderate, turn when firm enough, but slightly brown. Put on platter to cool. When cool enough to handle, spread with sardine butter and roll like a jelly roll. Roll in wax paper like kisses, place in lunch basket. A cream cheese could take the place of the sardines.

Cheese Souffle No. 1

1 cup bread crumbs	2 eggs
1 cup grated cheese	Salt and pepper to taste
1½ cups milk	

Heat milk just tepid, pour over crumbs and mix well. Add beaten eggs and all other ingredients, pour into a buttered baking dish and bake in moderate oven until firm (about 20 to 30 minutes), the time depending on the thickness or quantity.

Cheese Souffle No. 2

1 cup white sauce	1 teaspoon salt
1 cup grated cheese	⅛ teaspoon cayenne pepper
3 eggs	

Make white sauce; take from fire, add grated cheese, salt and pepper. Let cool while beating whites of eggs very stiff. When well beaten mix into cheese mixture the yolks slightly beaten. This will thin the mixture enough to pour over the stiff whites and fold in. Do this carefully; pour into a greased baking dish; place dish in pan of boiling water; put into a

moderate oven, bake 25 to 40 minutes. To test, insert handle of spoon through middle; if it comes out clean, it is done; if mixture sticks to handle, cook 5 to 7 minutes longer. Serve at once. Souffles, like omelets, must be eaten at once. They fall.

Corn Meal Souffle

1 pint sweet milk
¾ cup sifted meal
2 tablespoons butter

1 teaspoon salt
3 eggs

Heat milk in double boiler until smoking, but do not boil. Pour in meal slowly and cook until thick like a stiff white sauce. Take from fire to cool, add salt and butter. While the mixture is cooling, separate eggs and beat whites stiff, break yolks and add to meal mixture, then pour this mixture over stiff whites, fold in (do not beat), pour into a buttered pan, cook in moderate oven 25 to 30 minutes. When done serve at once from the pan in which it is baked. See Cheese Souffle No. 2 for testing when done.

Fish Souffle

Make same as cheese recipe, using one cup of flaked fish, cooked instead of cheese. Do not bake in water; use any seasoning liked.

Ham Souffle

Same as fish.

Chicken Souffle

Same as fish.

Oyster Souffle

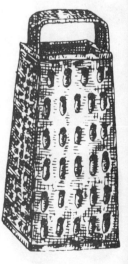

First steam the oysters in their own liquor until they curl slightly. Remove and drain; chop fine and use three-fourths cupful.

Make the white sauce, using half oyster liquor, half milk. Make as any souffle, using the three eggs. Season with salt, pepper, and a grated lemon rind, being careful to use only the yellow part, about one-half teaspoon. The amount of oysters used is less on account of the mixture measuring so solidly. Bake as directed until firm.

Corn Souffle

1 cup fresh or leftover corn
1 cup white sauce

3 eggs
Salt and pepper to taste

Make sauce as usual for medium thickness; add corn and let cool. Beat egg whites until stiff. Mix yolks into the corn mixture; add seasoning, fold in the whites.

Pour into a buttered pan and bake in a moderate oven about 25 minutes or until done. Test by inserting a spoon handle into center. If it comes out without the mixture sticking, it is done; if sticking, cook a little longer.

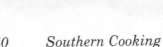

Squash Souffle

Make same as corn, using one cup of cooked and mashed squash.

Apple Souffle

3 cups stewed and strained apples   4 eggs
1 cup sugar   Season with spices to taste

Have apples free of lumps. Add sugar and spices while hot, let cool, beat egg together light, mix into apples. Pour into baking dish.
Bake until firm. Serve with roast pork.

Macaroni and Cheese

½ pound macaroni   ⅛ teaspoon cayenne pepper
1 cup cheese chips   ½ cup milk
3 tablespoons butter   1 egg
1 teaspoon salt   ½ cup buttered bread crumbs

Break and boil macaroni in salt water until tender (about 20 minutes). Blanch in cold water to prevent sticking. Cover bottom of baking dish with layer of macaroni, a sprinkle of cheese, bits of butter, salt and pepper.
Continue until all is used, having cheese on top.
Mix milk and egg together, pour over the dish, cover top with crumbs, bake in moderate oven long enough to brown top and cook egg and milk. Serve in the same dish.
A thin white sauce is someimes used instead of the milk and egg.
This dish, when left over, makes nice croquettes. Serve with tomato sauce.

Convent Pudding—Colonial Tea Room Recipe

½ cup macaroni   1 tablespoon chopped green pepper
1 cup milk   1 tablespoon onion juice
1 cup soft bread crumbs   1 tablespoon chopped parsley
¼ cup butter   3 eggs
1 cup grated cheese   1 teaspoon salt

Cook macaroni until tender. Scald milk, add all ingredients (eggs slightly beaten). Grease dish with butter, pour in mixture, place dish in boiling water with several thicknesses of paper at bottom and bake in boiling water for 30 to 40 minutes. Serve with tomato or mushroom sauce.

Cheese Custard

Cut sufficient layers of bread needed, spread with butter, sprinkle with cheese, salt and pepper; make two layers in baking dish, cover with 2 cups milk and 2 eggs beaten together. Bake half hour. Serve from dish in which it was baked.
Pepper and mustard may be added.

English Monkey

1 cup bread crumbs	1 egg
1 cup milk	½ teaspoon salt
½ cup soft cheese chips	⅛ teaspoon cayenne pepper
2 tablespoons of butter	

Soak the bread crumbs in the milk for fifteen minutes. Melt butter and cheese over a gentle heat. When melted, add soaked crumbs, the egg slightly beaten and seasonings. Cook 2 or 3 minutes. Pour over toasted crackers or bread, which has been slightly buttered, or serve from a hot dish with hot biscuit or wheat muffins.

"Ring Tum Ditty"

½ lb. American cheese	2 tablespoons flour
1 can tomato soup	1 teaspoon sugar
2 cups rich milk	Pinch soda
2 tablespoons butter	

Grate cheese, and when all ingredients are near a boiling point add the cheese. Care should be taken in not letting it boil. An onion and a pinch of mustard may be added. Serve over crackers or toast.

Cheese Sauce

1 cup white sauce	Salt and pepper to taste, using the
1 cup diced cheese	red pepper

Make white sauce, add the cheese, and stir until well melted and blended together. Pour into a hot dish to serve. This is good over rice, hominy, or toast. Also used to serve as a sauce over rice croquettes.

White Sauce

1 cup milk	2 tablespoons of butter
3 tablespoons of flour	Salt and pepper

Put milk into double boiler to heat. Into a saucepan place butter to melt. Add flour and blend together. When ready remove the saucepan from the fire, add the milk all at once and stir to thicken, then add cheese or serve as a sauce over any dish.

Cheese Jelly

Use recipe for Cheese Sauce. Add 2 tablespoons of gelatine dissolved in ¼ cup cold water, and add to sauce while hot and thoroughly melt. Let cool partly. Sprinkle well a layer cake pan with grated cheese. Pour the jelly in to congeal; when cold cut in squares, roll in grated cheese.

To be served with a salad.

Cheese and Potatoes

Boil, season and mash as many potatoes as needed, whip very light and mix one or more cups of grated cheese according to the quantity needed.

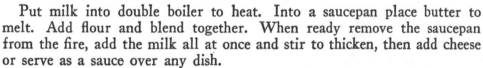

Pile on a shallow pan and bake until slightly browned and very hot, serve at once from the pan in which it is baked.

The potatoes may be baked, scooped from the skins. Season as above, refill the shells, bake just long enough to brown top and melt cheese. Serve with broiled fish.

Cheese Aigrettes

½ cup water	2 eggs and 1 yolk
¼ cup butter	¼ cup bottled Parmesan cheese
½ cup dry grated cheese	Salt and cayenne
½ cup flour	

Boil water and butter, add flour (as in making cream puffs), cook until it leaves the sides of pan. Cool slightly, add eggs one at a time and mix well. Lastily add the cheese. Drop in hot fat pieces as large as a walnut and fry a golden brown. Drain on paper and serve on a folded napkin.

Cheese Fritters

2 cups grated cheese	4 egg whites (½ cup)
3 tablespoons flour	Red pepper and salt

Mix flour, salt, pepper and cheese. Just before frying—beat egg whites very stiff and fold in cheese mixture. Dip a tablespoon of mixture each time and fry in deep fat. Drain on brown paper.

Cheese Balls

1 cup grated cheese	½ teaspoon salt
1 cup bread crumbs	Dash cayenne pepper
2 egg whites, beaten stiff	

Mix all ingredients together, make in balls the size of walnuts, fry in deep fat, drain, serve with salad.

Welsh Rarebit

1 lb. grated English dairy cheese	¾ cup milk
2 tablespoons butter	¼ cup cream
3 tablespoons flour	1 teaspoon salt
⅛ teaspoon cayenne pepper	

Melt butter in a saucepan or chafing dish, add flour and cook, without browning, until well mixed, stirring all the time; add milk and half of cheese, still stirring; when thoroughly heated and well mixed, add balance of cheese, being careful to stir all the time; when thick pour over nicely browned hot toast and serve.

Sweet Butter

1 lb. creamery butter	1 pint whole milk

Place butter in bowl and let soften to room temperature. Leave milk at room temperature until just cool. With a wire mixer or slitted spoon cream butter until soft and easy to stir. Add milk a little at a time, like

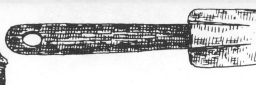

making mayonnaise, blending milk and butter until all the milk is added, and no milk is noticeable. Make in cottage prints. This will give 2 pounds of butter that will taste like fresh dairy butter. No more salt is added. Delicious.

Cottage Cheese

Allow the skimmed milk to clabber, over the clabbered milk pour hot water (not quite boiling), using about one quart of water to one quart of clabber. Allow it to stand until tepid.

Over a colander or strainer spread a cheese cloth, pour the mixture into this to drip, allowing it to drain until it is quite firm. Place in ice box to chill. Serve with sugar and cream, with a dash of nutmeg if liked. Served with salt, pepper and thick cream as a cheese.

Served with strawberry preserves this makes a nice dish.

Cheese Balls

To make cheese balls use cottage cheese, Neufchatel or Philadelphia cream. Moisten with thin cream or full milk to make a medium paste, add salt and cayenne pepper to taste. If any color is desired add now.

Make into small balls, roll in chopped parsley or chopped nuts. Fill celery stalks or use to make ribbon sandwiches.

Neufchatel Cheese Balls

Mash and make into a stiff paste two or three cakes of Neufchatel cheese using sweet cream or milk to moisten, season with plenty of salt and cayenne pepper, and make into balls the size of an English walnut. Press two halves of English walnut meats on each ball, place in ice box until very cold, serve with salad.

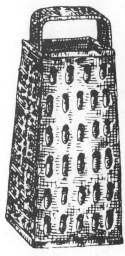

CHAPTER III

Vegetables

A Simple Classification of Vegetables
Succulent Vegetables

Those containing minerals, vitamins and those juicy in texture.

Turnip greens	Celery	Cucumbers
Mustard greens	Cabbage	Turnips
Spinach	Collards	Tomatoes
Kale	Asparagus	Eggplant
Chard	Brussels Sprouts	Okra
Watercress	Beets	Onions
Lettuce	Carrots	Parsnips
	Cauliflowers	Radishes

Carbohydrate Vegetables

Sweet corn	Irish potatoes
Squash	Sweet potatoes

Protein Vegetables

String beans	Kidney beans	Lady peas
Butterbeans	English peas	Field or blackeyed peas

Asparagus—Plain

Scrape, clean and boil asparagus in salt water till tender, about 30 minutes, drain and serve with white sauce or melted butter to which has been added salt, pepper and lemon juice. Have dish hot before putting asparagus in.

Fricasseed Asparagus

2 cups canned asparagus	1 head lettuce
1 small onion	1 tablespoon butter
2 tablespoons flour	1 cup of stock or milk

Make sauce of butter, flour and milk; chop asparagus in 1 inch pieces; cut lettuce rather coarse and pour both into sauce, season well with salt and pepper; add one egg and stir over a gentle fire about one minute, or until bound together and egg is cooked; serve at once.

Fresh Asparagus With Vinagrette Sauce

3 tablespoons melted butter or oil	1 tablespoon grated onion
1 tablespoon tarragon vinegar	1 teaspoon salt
2 tablespoons cider vinegar	½ teaspoon paprika
1 tablespoon chopped parsley	Cayenne pepper to suit taste

Melt butter; add vinegar and the seasonings; heat and pour hot over asparagus or cauliflower and serve immediately.

Canned Asparagus With Vinagrette Sauce

Open and heat the asparagus. Make and pour the sauce over, and serve.

French Fried Asparagus

Asparagus also lends itself to the French fry treatment. Drain the asparagus from its liquor, dip each stalk in fine crumbs, then into beaten egg, and into fine crumbs again. Drop in deep hot fat and fry to a golden brown. Dress with sweet pickled onions.

Cabbage

Cabbage should be boiled rapidly about 30 minutes in plenty of salted water in open pot, preferably without meat. At least when cooked without meat it is more digestible. Serve with melted butter or white sauce.

Lady Cabbage

1 cabbage (about 2 lbs.) cut in sections	2 eggs
	½ cup rich milk
1 tablespoon butter	¼ teaspoon white pepper
1 teaspoon salt	

Boil cabbage rapidly for 15 minutes, change water, have it boiling, and boil another 15 minutes, or till tender; drain and chop fine, add seasoning. Beat eggs light, add to the milk and then add to the cabbage; pour into a buttered baking dish and bake in a moderate oven from 20 to 30 minutes. If cooked too fast the eggs and milk will curdle. Cheese may be added if liked. Serve from the baking dish.

Stuffed Cabbage

1 medium cabbage (about 2 lbs.)	1 cup bread crumbs
1 cup pork sausage	1 egg
1 cup chopped cabbage	½ teaspoon salt

Cut cabbage from top towards stem half way into 8 sections and drop into warm water for 10 minutes. Fold back the sections leaving each section 4 or 5 leaves thick. scoop out center leaving an opening sufficient to hold stuffing. Chop cabbage removed; make a force meat of the ingredients called for and fill the cabbage. Bring the sections back over the stuffing, tie in cheese cloth. Drop in boiling water and cook for 1 hour. When done lift out and drain well; place on platter and pour over a cup of white sauce. Sprinkle with minced parsley or grated cheese and serve.

Hot Slaw

½ cup vinegar	¼ cup sugar or less
½ teaspoon mustard	2 teaspoons salad oil or butter
½ cup sweet cream or top milk	Salt and pepper to taste
1 egg	Cabbage

Shred 1 medium cabbage, boil in lots of water 15 minutes. Drain. Add hot dressing. Serve at once.

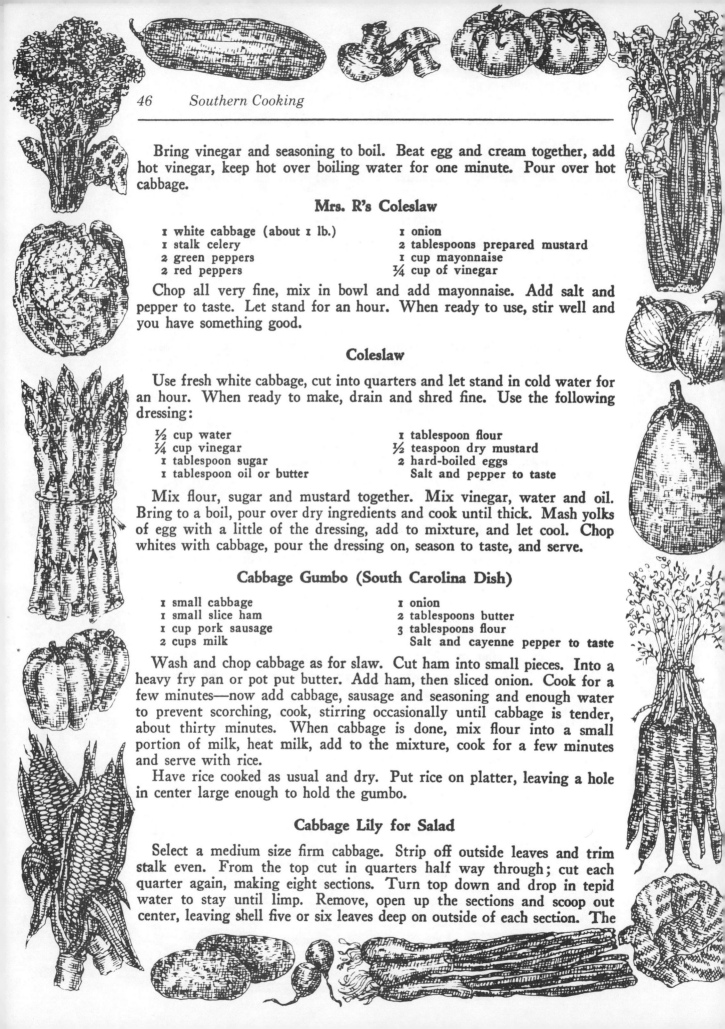

Bring vinegar and seasoning to boil. Beat egg and cream together, add hot vinegar, keep hot over boiling water for one minute. Pour over hot cabbage.

Mrs. R's Coleslaw

1 white cabbage (about 1 lb.)	1 onion
1 stalk celery	2 tablespoons prepared mustard
2 green peppers	1 cup mayonnaise
2 red peppers	¼ cup of vinegar

Chop all very fine, mix in bowl and add mayonnaise. Add salt and pepper to taste. Let stand for an hour. When ready to use, stir well and you have something good.

Coleslaw

Use fresh white cabbage, cut into quarters and let stand in cold water for an hour. When ready to make, drain and shred fine. Use the following dressing:

½ cup water	1 tablespoon flour
¼ cup vinegar	½ teaspoon dry mustard
1 tablespoon sugar	2 hard-boiled eggs
1 tablespoon oil or butter	Salt and pepper to taste

Mix flour, sugar and mustard together. Mix vinegar, water and oil. Bring to a boil, pour over dry ingredients and cook until thick. Mash yolks of egg with a little of the dressing, add to mixture, and let cool. Chop whites with cabbage, pour the dressing on, season to taste, and serve.

Cabbage Gumbo (South Carolina Dish)

1 small cabbage	1 onion
1 small slice ham	2 tablespoons butter
1 cup pork sausage	3 tablespoons flour
2 cups milk	Salt and cayenne pepper to taste

Wash and chop cabbage as for slaw. Cut ham into small pieces. Into a heavy fry pan or pot put butter. Add ham, then sliced onion. Cook for a few minutes—now add cabbage, sausage and seasoning and enough water to prevent scorching, cook, stirring occasionally until cabbage is tender, about thirty minutes. When cabbage is done, mix flour into a small portion of milk, heat milk, add to the mixture, cook for a few minutes and serve with rice.

Have rice cooked as usual and dry. Put rice on platter, leaving a hole in center large enough to hold the gumbo.

Cabbage Lily for Salad

Select a medium size firm cabbage. Strip off outside leaves and trim stalk even. From the top cut in quarters half way through; cut each quarter again, making eight sections. Turn top down and drop in tepid water to stay until limp. Remove, open up the sections and scoop out center, leaving shell five or six leaves deep on outside of each section. The opening should be large enough to hold a quart or more of salad. With scissors cut each section into still smaller strips like long slim petals or leaves as deep as the first cutting, still leaving the lower part intact. Into a large deep dishpan or lard can filled with cold or ice water sufficient to float the cabbage, drop cabbage cut side down. Let stay several hours until it opens out, curls and becomes very crisp. Drain well; place in glass bowl or on platter and fill center with salad. Garnish petals with strips of pimentoes and rings of stuffed olives. Any garnishing sprinkled over top will be pretty.

Brussels Sprouts

Remove any withered leaves and drop into cold water to freshen. Cook and season the same as cauliflower or cabbage.

Cauliflower

Strip off the coarse green stalks and trim neatly near the flower. Drop in cold salt water for 20 to 30 minutes; then drop into boiling salt water and cook until tender. Drain and serve with melted butter or white sauce.

The large flower may be broken into small pieces (flowerets) if preferred. Cook uncovered and rapidly.

To Clean Spinach

Use a large vessel and have plenty of water. Do not crowd the pan. Take a large handful at a time, shake and dip up and down into the water, thus shaking off the grit which goes to the bottom of the pan. Change the water (and rinse the pan well) four or five times until clean. New Zealand spinach is usually not very gritty.

To Cook Spinach

Pick, wash and drain the required amount of spinach. Put the spinach into a kettle or saucepan without any water, have a moderate fire. In a few minutes the spinach will wilt and send out sufficient water to cook it Boil for 20 to 30 minutes briskly so the water will be reduced, season with butter, chop fine, garnish with eggs and serve.

Plain Spinach

Wash and cook half peck of spinach, as directed above. Drain well, chop fine or put through a coarse sieve. Fry two or three slices of bacon, remove and into the grease put spinach and season with the grease, add salt and pepper to taste, a small amount of vinegar if liked. Serve as any greens.

To Cooked Canned Spinach

Open a can of spinach and turn into a sauce pan of cold water. Stir with a fork to loosen well; let it stand about thirty minutes.

Take out of water with a skimmer; drain well; heat in a small quantity

of water or butter until done (about ten minutes). Season with salt, pepper, and serve.

A Mold of Spinach

2 cups spinach	Salt and pepper to taste
1 cup white sauce	Onion, catsup, paprika, if desired
3 eggs	

Cook, drain and chop the spinach or put through a coarse sieve, then measure. Make and add the white sauce. Beat eggs together until well broken, add to spinach, but do not let the mixture be hot enough to cook the eggs.

Butter a border mold generously with soft (not melted) butter, pour in the mixture until ¾ full. Place mold in pan of boiling water and steam until firm. Inside the oven or top of stove may be used. Cover top lightly to prevent browning if oven is used.

Use a baking pan for steaming, putting several thicknesses of paper on bottom to protect the bottom of mold which is the top when turned out. Have water half or three-fourths the depth of mold so it will not boil over into mold.

Individual molds may be used, standing them in hot water the same as any other. Turn out (the same as any mold or jelly) onto hot platter, serve with grated cheese, eggs or carrots. More white sauce may be poured over the mold. Small Irish potatoes with white sauce filled in the center make a very attractive dish.

Spinach Souffle

2 cups cooked spinach	1 cup milk
2 tablespoons butter	4 tablespoons flour
3 eggs	Salt and pepper to taste

Chop spinach fine and put through coarse strainer; make milk, butter and flour into white sauce; add spinach; let cool enough not to cook yolks of eggs, which should be beaten and added. Whip whites stiff and fold into mixture. Pour into a buttered baking dish and cook in a moderate oven 25 minutes, or until firm.

Broiled Spinach

Select crisp leaves of fresh spinach. Into a fry pan put butter or bacon drippings; then put in leaves, turn, cooking on both sides for a few minutes. Lift carefully to a plate and serve piping hot.

Turnip Greens

Turnip greens should be thoroughly washed to be free of grit. Remove any objectionable part of tough stems. For ½ peck of greens use just enough water to cover ¼ lb. seasoning meat. Bring meat and water to a boil, add greens and bring to a hard boil, then lower heat and cook slowly for 2 hours or until tender, and water reduced to about a cup.

Young, tender greens cook in less time than older plants.

Greens should not be greasy but tasty and seasoned. More salt may be added if necessary. If too much water is used much of the food value is lost (left in the liquor).

All kinds of greens are cooked as turnip greens in this section of the South.

Chard

Beet tops, swiss chard and spinach may be cooked as turnip greens, or put into a pot without water. Cook slowly for a few minutes until enough water has come from the leaves to do the cooking. Cook moderately about 30 minutes. Drain, chop, season with salt, pepper, melted butter or white sauce.

Kale

Cook the same as turnip greens.

Swiss Chard

Cook leaves as greens or spinach.

Cook stalks. Boil in salt water until tender; serve with melted butter or white sauce.

Rape

See Kale.

Mustard

Mustard is used mixed with other greens and cooked the same as turnip greens.

Curly mustard is used for garnishing the same as parsley.

Collards

The blue and white stem collards are strictly a southern vegetable, and not good until the frost and cold have made them brittle and tender. The leaf is dark green with a large, thick stem running through the center about half the length of leaf.

Collards are boiled with seasoning meat or ham hock about 2 hours. They must be boiled slowly, and kept well under water.

Collard Sprouts

After the collard has been cut and used the stalk if left standing will in the spring send out very tender sprouts. These sprouts are cooked the same as collards, not requiring as long cooking or as much water.

Collard Stalks

Strip off the leafy part and cut stalks in 1 inch pieces. Boil until tender in salt water. Drain and serve with melted butter or white sauce.

Snap Beans

String snap beans should be cooked with boiling meat slowly from 2 to 3 hours. Use ⅛ pound of meat for a quart of beans. Cover with water and when boiled slowly the water is not condensed too fast. There should be about one cup full when done.

If beans are boiled rapidly and water added often they are never as good. Rapid cooking tears them open and causes them to be "stringy." Start in boiling water.

To String Beans

Break off blossom end first towards inside curve, pull string down to stem end. Break small piece from stem end and pull off string back to starting end. Break in several pieces and drop into cold water to freshen. All vegetables are improved in flavor if crisped or dropped into cold water before cooking.

Southern people prefer most vegetables being cooked with a piece of meat instead of serving with butter or cream.

Vegetables should not be too heavily salted as it destroys the flavor.

Barbecued String Beans

3 cups beans	1 tablespoon prepared mustard
4 tablespoons butter	1 teaspoon curry powder (optional)
1 tablespoon minced onion	1 teaspoon prepared horseradish
1 tablespoon minced pepper	1 teaspoon salt
¼ cup chili sauce	⅛ teaspoon red pepper
¼ cup vinegar	1½ cups boiling water

Cook beans in salt water until tender and done. Melt butter in fry pan, add onions and pepper and cook until done. Add all seasoning and hot water, cook five minutes before adding beans. Simmer slowly until beans are well seasoned. Serve.

Butterbeans

Shell and remove any faulty beans, use twice as much water (cold) as beans. Boil gently until tender and water is almost cooked away. Add salt, butter and small portion of sweet cream. Some prefer a piece of seasoning meat to cook with beans instead of butter.

Lima Beans

Cook the same as butterbeans. As these are a larger and somewhat coarser variety, longer cooking will perhaps be required.

Dried Lima Beans

Wash, pick out faulty beans and soak in cold water over night. When ready to cook cover with cold water and bring to a boil gradually. Drain and cover with boiling water, and cook until tender. A small piece of seasoning meat or butter may be used in cooking.

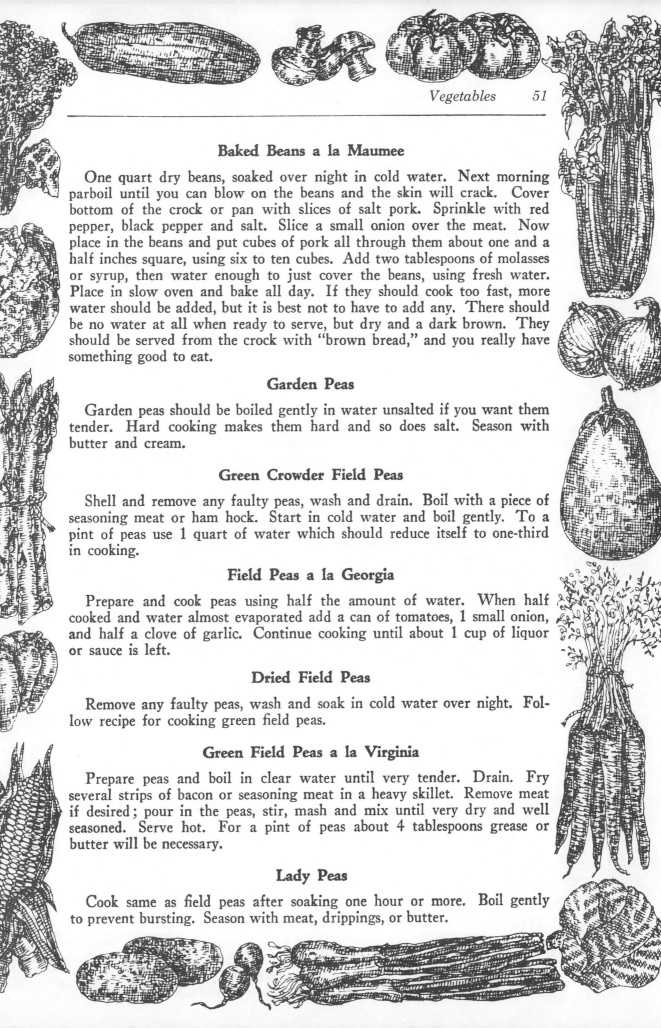

Baked Beans a la Maumee

One quart dry beans, soaked over night in cold water. Next morning parboil until you can blow on the beans and the skin will crack. Cover bottom of the crock or pan with slices of salt pork. Sprinkle with red pepper, black pepper and salt. Slice a small onion over the meat. Now place in the beans and put cubes of pork all through them about one and a half inches square, using six to ten cubes. Add two tablespoons of molasses or syrup, then water enough to just cover the beans, using fresh water. Place in slow oven and bake all day. If they should cook too fast, more water should be added, but it is best not to have to add any. There should be no water at all when ready to serve, but dry and a dark brown. They should be served from the crock with "brown bread," and you really have something good to eat.

Garden Peas

Garden peas should be boiled gently in water unsalted if you want them tender. Hard cooking makes them hard and so does salt. Season with butter and cream.

Green Crowder Field Peas

Shell and remove any faulty peas, wash and drain. Boil with a piece of seasoning meat or ham hock. Start in cold water and boil gently. To a pint of peas use 1 quart of water which should reduce itself to one-third in cooking.

Field Peas a la Georgia

Prepare and cook peas using half the amount of water. When half cooked and water almost evaporated add a can of tomatoes, 1 small onion, and half a clove of garlic. Continue cooking until about 1 cup of liquor or sauce is left.

Dried Field Peas

Remove any faulty peas, wash and soak in cold water over night. Follow recipe for cooking green field peas.

Green Field Peas a la Virginia

Prepare peas and boil in clear water until very tender. Drain. Fry several strips of bacon or seasoning meat in a heavy skillet. Remove meat if desired; pour in the peas, stir, mash and mix until very dry and well seasoned. Serve hot. For a pint of peas about 4 tablespoons grease or butter will be necessary.

Lady Peas

Cook same as field peas after soaking one hour or more. Boil gently to prevent bursting. Season with meat, drippings, or butter.

To Cook Squash

Select tender squash, scrub, remove ends and cut in slices; boil in salt water until tender. Drain. Into a fry pan put bacon drippings, butter, or butter substitute, pour in the squash, mash and cook until all water is dried out. Season with pepper, a little onion and more salt if necessary. There should be no grease evident, yet plenty to season.

A little flour sprinkled into squash while cooking is a binder and improves the dish (about 2 tablespoons to a medium dish).

If squash are old, peel and remove large seed or put through a food chopper.

Yellow squash are considered better than white, although both are grown and prepared the same way.

Squash Cakes

1 cup leftover squash	2 tablespoons flour
1 egg	

Mix together, add enough sweet milk to make the consistency of batter cakes, and cook as such or fry as a fritter in shallow grease. Serve hot.

This makes a nice luncheon dish.

Plain Squash Souffle

2 cups squash cooked, mashed and measured	3 tablespoons bacon drippings or butter
1 cup dry bread crumbs	2 eggs
1 cup milk	Salt and pepper to taste
1 tablespoon grated onion	

Melt butter in hot milk; pour over bread crumbs, mix well, add to squash. Add seasoning, beat eggs all together and add to mixture. Pour into a baking dish and bake 20 to 30 minutes in moderate oven. Serve from the dish. The top may be covered with buttered crumbs, using extra crumbs for topping.

Squash Souffle

1 cup white sauce	1 teaspoon salt
1 cup mashed squash (left over)	White or cayenne pepper to taste
3 eggs	

Make white sauce, using an extra portion of flour, one to two tablespoons, to have it quite stiff. Add squash to sauce while hot. This heats the squash and cools the sauce. Add seasoning. Separate eggs, beat whites stiff. When ready, mix the yolks into the sauce and squash mixture, then fold into the whites. Pour into a buttered pan, bake in a moderate oven 30 minutes. To test insert knife or spoon handle into the center. If it comes out clean it is done; if sticky, cook longer. Serve in the pan in which it was baked. It must be served at once.

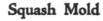

Squash Mold

2 cups of mashed squash
1 cup thick white sauce
3 eggs

1 teaspoon grated onion
Salt and pepper to taste

Steam or boil the squash until tender, drain well and put through a coarse sieve. Mix and fill mold. See directions for Spinach Mold.

Stuffed Squashes

Select tender, yellow squashes of uniform size, about as large around as a tumbler. Cut a small slice from the blossom end and then cut off the neck, leaving the body of uniform size. Cut in half crosswise. This gives the cup-shaped pieces. With a spoon scoop out the inside, leaving the walls and bottom about one-fourth of an inch thick. Have the large end for the top. Put into salt water and boil until tender. Lift out and drain. Cook the part scooped out, the ends and as much more as will be needed. Steam or boil in salt water until tender; drain, mash, add any seasoning liked—onions, peppers, butter, cream or bacon drippings. Cook until dry. Sometimes a small portion of flour will hold together; fill the cups; cover the tops with buttered crumbs; put into a greased pan and bake until the crumbs are a golden brown. The squashes will retain their yellow look.

Serve on a platter or individually.

Scalloped Squash

Follow recipe for Eggplant. Grated onion is an improvement to squash.

To Stew Corn

6 ears corn
¾ cup water
½ cup sweet milk or cream

3 tablespoons butter or bacon drippings

Select full tender corn. Shuck and remove silks. With a knife split each row of grains. Cut off about one-third of the grain all around. Repeat the cutting and then scrape the remaining pulp.

This gives a fine cut corn.

Add water. Put grease into a saucepan and make hot. Pour in the corn and stir constantly until hot. Lower the fire and cook slowly for 30 minutes. Heat and add milk, salt and pepper. Mix well and it is ready to serve. Sometimes there is more starch in the corn and it thickens more or less. Add more or less water to suit. Have the consistency to eat with a fork.

Corn should be cooked from twenty to forty minutes. That depends on the age and quantity. Too much and too long heat will toughen corn.

Usually the canned vegetables require very little cooking.

To Boil Corn on Cob

Have water boiling, drop in the corn and bring to a boil, lower heat

so it will boil gently for 10 or 15 minutes. Cover pot. When done lift out, drain, send to table either in a covered dish or covered with a napkin. Each person puts his own salt, pepper and butter on as eaten. If you like, split the grains when it comes from the pot before sending to table.

Steamed Corn

Place ears of corn in a colander over boiling water, cover colander. Boil water hard to steam corn until done (about 30 minutes).

Miss Phoebe's Corn on Cob

Prepare tender corn, amount needed, place ears in a large saucepan and cover with cold water. Place over fire; bring water just to boil; remove from fire and allow corn to stand in hot water for 10 or 15 minutes. If corn is quite large let stand a little longer.

Remove from water and serve.

A tablespoon of sugar may be added to water if liked—never any salt.

Fried Corn

3 cups of cut corn	2 teaspoons salt
3 tablespoons butter or bacon drippings	⅛ teaspoon pepper

Into a heavy skillet put grease and get very hot, add corn and cook about 20 minutes. Stir often to prevent scorching. This will be thick and some parts brown.

Corn Pudding

2 cups corn	2 tablespoons flour
1 cup sweet milk	1 tablespoon sugar
2 tablespoons butter	3 eggs
2 teaspoons salt	Red or white pepper to taste

Cut corn as usual or use left over. Add all the seasonings. Beat eggs together until light, put into the mixture, pour into a buttered baking dish and bake in a moderate oven.

If it is cooked too fast, the custard or milk and egg will curdle. It should be firm, like a cup custard.

Place dish with pudding into a pan of boiling water and it will cook slower. Serve in the dish in which it is cooked. By warming the milk it will cook quicker.

South Carolina Corn Pudding

4 or 5 ears of well-filled but tender corn	2 eggs
	2 tablespoons butter
1 pint sweet milk heated until warm	Salt, pepper

Grate the corn on vegetable or coconut grater. Beat eggs, add to corn, add milk and melted butter, salt, pepper; mix well. Bake in greased pan, preferably greased with cooking oil, in moderate oven, about 25 minutes, until well set, but do not let it reach boiling temperature or the eggs and milk will separate. This may sound like any other corn pudding, but the grating is what makes it "different."

The pan may be set in boiling water to prevent over-cooking.

This will serve six persons.

Corn Pudding au Gratin

2 cups canned corn	1 cup milk
1 cup diced cheese	1 tablespoon sugar
2 tablespoons flour	2 tablespoons butter
1 teaspoon salt	$\frac{1}{8}$ teaspoon pepper
2 eggs	$\frac{1}{2}$ cup bread crumbs (buttered)

Add cheese, flour, sugar and other seasoning to corn and mix well. Beat eggs; add to corn. Heat milk, add to mixture; pour into greased baking dish and cover top with crumbs. Bake until firm.

Serve in pan in which it is cooked.

Corn Souffle

1 cup fresh or leftover corn	3 eggs
1 cup white sauce	Salt and pepper to taste

Make sauce as usual for medium thickness; add corn and let cool. Beat egg whites until stiff. Mix yolks into the corn mixture; add seasoning, fold in whites.

Pour into a buttered pan and bake in a moderate oven about 25 minutes or until done. Test by inserting a spoon handle into center. If it comes out without the mixture sticking, it is done; if sticking, cook a little longer.

Green Corn Spoon Bread

2 cups milk	2 teaspoons sugar
$\frac{1}{3}$ cup corn meal	1 teaspoon salt
3 ears corn cut very fine	4 tablespoons butter
2 eggs, beaten separately	

Bring to a boil 1 cup of the milk, add corn and the meal, stirring constantly and cook for five minutes. Remove from the fire and beat in butter, sugar, salt and the rest of the milk, which is cold and this cools the mixture. Add beaten yolks, then fold in stiffly beaten whites. Pour in buttered dish or pan and bake 30 minutes in moderate oven. Serve with fried chicken or lamb chops.

Scalloped Corn and Tomatoes

Put a layer of corn into a baking pan; then a layer of bread crumbs, dot with butter, salt and pepper. Put a layer of sliced tomatoes, season as the crumbs (with butter, salt and pepper). Continue with alternate layers of corn, crumbs and tomatoes until pan is full, having crumbs on top. Bake in moderate oven 30 minutes or until crumbs are brown. Serve in dish in which it was baked.

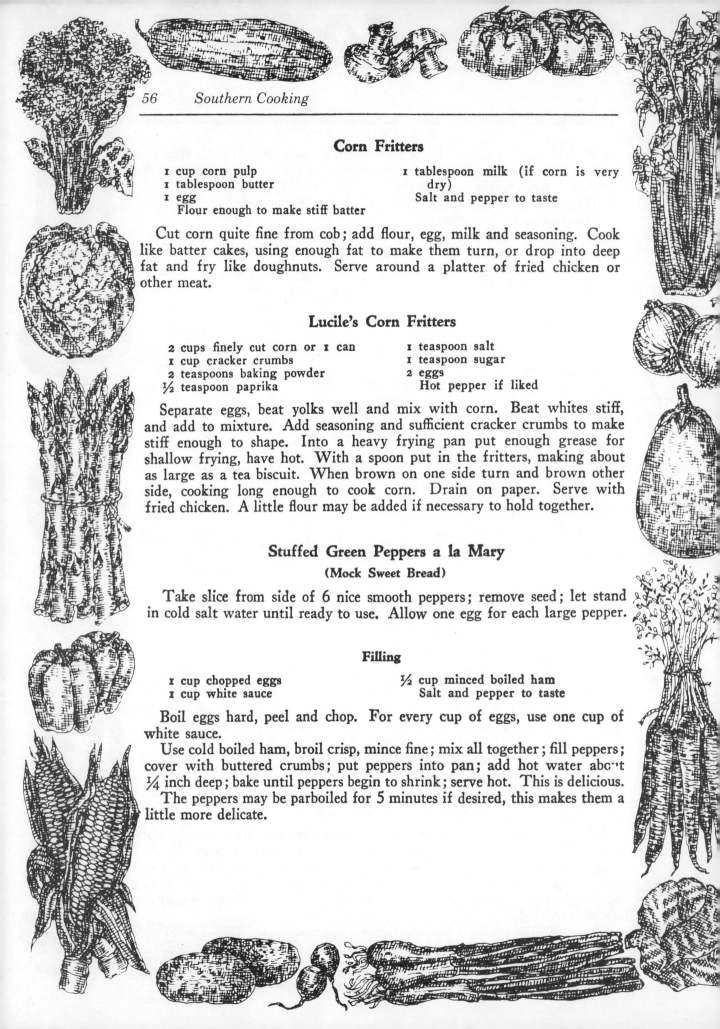

Corn Fritters

1 cup corn pulp
1 tablespoon butter
1 egg
    Flour enough to make stiff batter

1 tablespoon milk (if corn is very dry)
Salt and pepper to taste

Cut corn quite fine from cob; add flour, egg, milk and seasoning. Cook like batter cakes, using enough fat to make them turn, or drop into deep fat and fry like doughnuts. Serve around a platter of fried chicken or other meat.

Lucile's Corn Fritters

2 cups finely cut corn or 1 can
1 cup cracker crumbs
2 teaspoons baking powder
½ teaspoon paprika

1 teaspoon salt
1 teaspoon sugar
2 eggs
Hot pepper if liked

Separate eggs, beat yolks well and mix with corn. Beat whites stiff, and add to mixture. Add seasoning and sufficient cracker crumbs to make stiff enough to shape. Into a heavy frying pan put enough grease for shallow frying, have hot. With a spoon put in the fritters, making about as large as a tea biscuit. When brown on one side turn and brown other side, cooking long enough to cook corn. Drain on paper. Serve with fried chicken. A little flour may be added if necessary to hold together.

Stuffed Green Peppers a la Mary

(Mock Sweet Bread)

Take slice from side of 6 nice smooth peppers; remove seed; let stand in cold salt water until ready to use. Allow one egg for each large pepper.

Filling

1 cup chopped eggs
1 cup white sauce

½ cup minced boiled ham
Salt and pepper to taste

Boil eggs hard, peel and chop. For every cup of eggs, use one cup of white sauce.

Use cold boiled ham, broil crisp, mince fine; mix all together; fill peppers; cover with buttered crumbs; put peppers into pan; add hot water about ¼ inch deep; bake until peppers begin to shrink; serve hot. This is delicious.

The peppers may be parboiled for 5 minutes if desired, this makes them a little more delicate.

A New Stuffed Pepper

Remove a slice from side of pepper, take out seed and white sections, but leave stem on. Parboil for 5 minutes and drain well. Make the following mixture:

1 cup bread crumbs	1 small onion
2 tablespoons butter	Salt, pepper and catsup

Melt butter, mince onion and fry until brown; remove from fire, add crumbs and mix well. Into each pepper put 1 tablespoon crumbs. Place peppers in baking dish, break an egg into each pepper, cover with more of the seasoned crumbs, filling pepper full. Bake in moderate oven for 10 minutes or until egg is cooked

Stuffed Peppers

1 cup cooked carrots	2 tablespoons butter or drippings
1 cup white turnips	1 teaspoon grated onion
1 cup bread crumbs	Enough sweet milk to moisten
1 egg	

Cook carrots and turnips in boiling salt water, add as much sugar as salt used. Mix all ingredients together, season, stuff peppers, cover top with buttered crumbs. Bake just long enough to brown on top.

Filling for Green Peppers

1 cup cold rice	1 teaspoon salt
½ cup cold diced meat	Any kind of flavoring liked
2 tablespoons butter	

Moisten with canned or fresh tomatoes, fill peppers; cover top with buttered crumbs; cook in a moderate oven 30 minutes, or till tender or brown; serve hot.

Peppers may be parboiled if preferred.

Green Peppers as a Relish

Wash and place on ice to crisp. Slice, remove seed and serve with salad, or as a raw vegetable.

To Cook Okra

Wash well and trim stem end, leaving enough of the pod to keep the juices in that the mucilage does not come out. Cover with boiling water and boil gently until tender. When half done, add salt. When ready to serve, drain, pour into a hot dish and add melted butter sufficient to season. A bit of lemon juice or vinegar is liked by some over the okra when eating.

To cook okra with a piece of boiling meat in place of using butter is a favorite way with many.

Boiled Okra

Select tender pods of okra of uniform size, about 2½ inches long. Remove stems but do not cut into pod. Boil in salted water until tender but not soft.

Serve with Hollandaise sauce.

Fried Okra

Select small, tender pods.

Boil until tender, drain, season with salt and pepper, roll in crumbs, then in egg and crumb again. Fry in deep fat. This is crumbed and egged the same as a croquette.

To Fry Okra

Cut into half-inch slices, crosswise; sprinkle generously with meal and fry in grease like French fried potatoes. Sprinkle with salt; serve hot.

Georgia Gumbo

¼ cup bacon drippings	1 quart of cup okra
1 large onion	1 cup of boiling water
6 fresh tomatoes, peeled and sliced	Salt and pepper to taste

Into a heavy fry pan put grease; slice onion quite thin and fry in grease a very light brown. Care must be taken not to burn or cook too much, for this would ruin the entire dish. Add tomatoes, okra and water; stir often; add seasoning when half done.

Cook about 1 hour. The mixture should be thick enough to be eaten with a fork. Serve with dry rice or as a vegetable with small individual corn meal hoe cakes, which should be well done and crusty.

Half a dozen fresh mushrooms broiled, chopped and added would make the dish more delicious. To rub the pan with a cut clove of garlic gives another added charm.

This mixture prepared and put into green peppers and baked would be another way of using.

Okra Gumbo

1 quart diced okra	1 clove of garlic
3 strips breakfast bacon	1 green pepper (seed removed)
3 tomatoes	6 stuffed olives
1 onion	Salt and pepper to taste

Wash and cut okra, cut all vegetables into rather fine pieces, peeling tomatoes before cutting. Fry bacon until crisp, remove and mince. Into fry pan put okra, onion, olives and pepper and cook until seared but not burned, add tomatoes and cook slowly until done, about 30 minutes. When served sprinkle minced bacon and parsley over top of dish. Serve with dry rice or toast points.

Scalloped Eggplant

Slice, peel and boil in salted water until tender one medium size eggplant. Drain and chop.

Into a baking dish put a layer of eggplant, bits of butter and a sprinkle of black pepper, then a layer of crushed crackers, until all is used, having eggplant on the top.

Mix one egg with one cup of milk and pour over the dish, using just enough to peep through the top. Cover top with buttered crumbs. Bake in medium oven until crumbs are brown and milk and egg are cooked, about 30 minutes, serve from dish in which it was cooked. Use oyster or snowflake crackers. An extra egg makes the dish richer.

Stuffed Eggplant

Select a good sized eggplant; cut a good slice from the side leaving large enough to fill and serve from. Remove the inside, leaving the rind intact. Boil the eggplant in salt water until done; drain, season with butter or bacon drippings, salt and pepper; add a little milk, one egg and a few bread crumbs. Return to the shell, cover the opening with buttered crumbs and bake until they are a good brown and long enough to cook the egg.

Baked Eggplant

Peel, boil, mash and let cool enough eggplant to make about two cups. Season with salt, pepper to taste. Beat 2 eggs together well; add 4 tablespoons of milk, 2 tablespoons of melted butter. Mix with the eggplant, pour into a buttered baking dish; cover top with buttered crumbs.

Use a moderate oven. Bake just long enough to cook the eggs and brown the top; about 20 minutes. Sometimes the rind of the eggplant is used in place of a pan. Cut a slice from side or end, scoop out the inside, boil and when seasoned refill the shell and bake. Place on a platter and garnish the dish.

Eggplant Janet

Remove a slice from the side of an eggplant, scoop out and boil pulp until tender, drain. Mix with 1 cup of white sauce, ¼ cup grated cheese, ½ cup cold meat, ground. Cover top with buttered crumbs, bake until brown. Serve from the shell.

Broiled Eggplant

Peel and slice plant ¾ inch thick—let stand in cold water 15 minutes, drain and wrap in towel to dry. Broil exactly as you would a steak, turning and browning until tender. Put on hot platter, season with salt, melted butter, and a good sprinkling of lemon juice. Serve.

Fried Eggplant

Peel and cut in ¼ inch slices crosswise. Soak slices in salt water 30 minutes; drain, and wipe dry. Dip each slice in flour, then in beaten egg and then cracker crumbs. Cook in deep fat like a croquette only a little less rapidly, giving time to cook slice thoroughly. Drain on paper and serve hot.

Eggplant Fritters

1 egg	1 medium (or 1 cup) eggplant
2 teaspoons baking powder	1 tablespoon butter
2 tablespoons flour	

Peel, slice and cook the eggplant in salt water until tender; drain and mash. There should be about 1 cup. Add beaten egg, butter and flour. Drop into hot grease and fry until brown, or cook like cakes, using just enough grease to turn them.

Eggplant Souffle

1 medium eggplant boiled and mashed fine	1 cup bread crumbs
1 tablespoon butter	1 onion
¼ cup milk	2 eggs
	Salt and pepper to taste

Mix all ingredients together, cover top with the bread crumbs and bake in moderate oven 30 to 40 minutes.

Tomatoes

It was not many years ago that no thought was given to the food value of tomatoes. Only the seasoning put in them counted, and all tomatoes were small in size. But the cultivation and improvements by Luther Burbank and his followers have brought about an increase in size of tomatoes and now some of them are so large they are called "beefsteak" tomatoes.

Today tomatoes are a necessary food. They supply us the much talked-of vitamins which food experts tell us we must have to keep fit.

The juice of fresh or canned tomatoes is the best substitute known for orange juice, which is so essential to babies fed on artificial food and to invalids.

Tomatoes, like oranges, contain stored up sunshine, that is when they are gathered ripe. It is the warm sunshine that develops or makes vita-

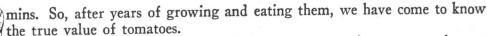

mins. So, after years of growing and eating them, we have come to know the true value of tomatoes.

Tomatoes are colorful and beautiful and have enough tartness to sharpen the appetite.

Then, too, tomatoes help the housewife to change many a dish. There are numberless ways of using, from the first course, as an appetizer, soup, vegetable and salad.

Raw Tomatoes

Select ripe tomatoes. Peel with a small paring knife just through the skin. Chill, slice in half inch slices or serve whole (cutting into eight sections half way through the tomato pulling sections slightly open). Have blossom end up. Serve with salt, pepper and vinegar; French dressing or mayonnaise.

When placed on lettuce it then serves as a salad.

Broiled Tomatoes

Select firm, ripe tomatoes. Peel and cut crosswise in slices half an inch thick. Drain for a minute; dip in flour. Into a heavy fry pan put 2 tablespoons butter. Heat and broil tomatoes on both sides until brown. Turn with batter cake turner. Serve with broiled fish, steak, or poached eggs.

Stewed Tomatoes No. 1

1 can or 1 quart of tomatoes	1 teaspoon sugar
2 tablespoons bread crumbs	1 teaspoon salt
2 tablespoons butter	Dash of pepper

Stew tomatoes in their own juice until thick and done. Add seasoning and serve. Some prefer to leave out bread crumbs.

Stewed Tomatoes No. 2

Stew tomatoes as directed in above recipe leaving out bread crumbs. Have 2 cups of toasted bread cubes about size of 1 inch, and when tomatoes are thick put toasted cubes in dish; pour hot tomatoes over them and serve.

Grilled Tomatoes

3 large tomatoes	1 green pepper
6 slices of bacon	1 white onion
6 rounds of toast	1 cup grated yellow cheese

Run the pepper and onion through the food chopper. Place tomatoes in boiling water for 5 minutes, then slip off the skins and cut in half. Cut the bread in rounds a little larger than the tomatoes, and toast them. Place a half tomato on each round of toast. Place a heaping tablespoon of pepper and onion on each tomato, salt well, and top with a heaping tablespoon of grated cheese. Place on a baking sheet under a broiler flame

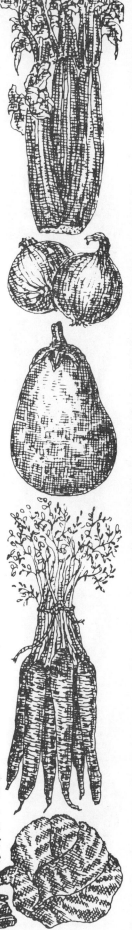

until the cheese melts and browns. Garnish with crisp bacon and stuffed olives.

Tomatoes and Macaroni

6 medium sized tomatoes	2 tablespoons grated cheese
¾ cup cooked macaroni	3 tablespoons bread crumbs
½ cup white sauce	Salt and pepper to taste

From stem end take a slice from each tomato. Scoop out the inside, salt and invert to drain. Cook the portion taken out until quite thick, mix with the white sauce. Cut macaroni in short pieces, add seasoning, fill tomatoes, put crumbs over top. Place in a greased pan, bake in moderate oven 20 to 30 minutes, until tomato is done and top is brown.

Creamed Tomatoes

Peel and cut thick slices of tomatoes, broil in lard or butter, place on platter, cover with cream sauce, sprinkle top with cheese.

Stuffed Tomatoes

6 medium tomatoes	1 cup cold rice, hominy or bread
2 tablespoons of butter or bacon grease	crumbs
1 tablespoon chopped onion	½ cup buttered crumbs
	Salt and pepper to taste

Select tomatoes of uniform size and from the stem end cut a slice; remove seed and part of the pulp, sprinkle with salt and invert to drain. Into a saucepan put the butter and onion and cook slightly, then add the tomato pulp and continue cooking for about ten minutes. Add the seasoning, cold rice and mix well, having it rather stiff; fill the tomato shells and cover the tops with the buttered crumbs. Place in a greased pan; add just enough water to prevent sticking to the bottom; bake in moderate oven about 20 minutes.

Tomato Timbales

1 quart of tomatoes (canned or fresh)	1 teaspoon salt
	1 tablespoon sugar
1 small onion	2 whole cloves

Boil until done, about ten minutes; put through a coarse sieve. There should be 2 cups. Add a half cup of stale bread crumbs and mix well. When cool, add 2 eggs slightly beaten and blend all together.

Pour into buttered timbale molds, place in boiling water and bake until firm. Place on several folds of paper before adding the water. Unmold on hot platter, pour cheese sauce over all, sprinkle with chopped parsley, and serve.

For cheese sauce make the usual white sauce, add a cup of grated cheese, blend together until cheese is well melted.

Tomatoes a la Schreiber at Breakfast Time

3 good sized firm tomatoes
1 cup white sauce

6 slices of buttered toast

Peel and slice each tomato in about three slices. Make and butter slightly the toast. Into a skillet put enough butter to broil the tomatoes and when this is done make the white sauce in the same pan adding more butter if necessary. As the tomatoes are broiled lay on the pieces of toast and place in a platter. Make the white sauce, pour over all, garnish with parsley and serve piping hot.

Tomato Rarebit

½ pound cheese chipped fine
1 can tomato soup (medium size)

Salt and pepper to taste

Heat slowly all together in double boiler, stir to mix well. Serve over hot buttered toast.

Baked Tomatoes

6 tomatoes
2 teaspoons salt
1 tablespoon butter
1 cup stock or milk

4 slices of bacon or the drippings
2 tablespoons flour
Pepper to taste

Cut tomatoes in halves without peeling, place in a baking dish with the cut side up making cups of the tomatoes, sprinkle with salt and pepper, cut the bacon and put a piece on each piece of tomato; bake in a moderate oven for 20 to 30 minutes; when done put on a platter and make a brown sauce as follows:

Melt butter, add flour and allow to brown, now add stock making a smooth sauce; mash one of the cooked tomatoes in the sauce, using any juice or brown part that accumulated in cooking, pour over the tomatoes and serve. Any seasoning liked may be added to the sauce; more bacon may be broiled and served crisp around the platter, which makes a heavier dish. Mushrooms added to the sauce would still increase the food value and would be a delicious luncheon dish fit for the king.

Scalloped Tomatoes

6 tomatoes
4 strips bacon
2 hard-boiled eggs
2 cups oyster crackers

½ cup hot water
½ cup bread crumbs
Salt and pepper

Broil and mince bacon, saving the drippings for seasoning. Peel and slice tomatoes, putting in a layer of tomatoes, a part of minced bacon and one egg, sliced thin. Add salt and pepper, then a layer of crushed crackers. Continue until all is used, having tomatoes on top.

Add bacon drippings to hot water and pour over all. Cover top with the crumbs, bake until brown. A green pepper or small onion is a nice flavor for a change.

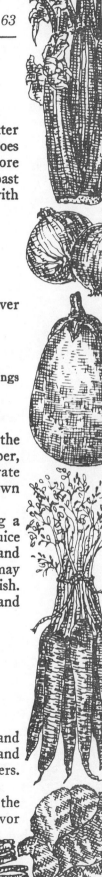

Tomato Mayonnaise

1 cup of mayonnaise   Salt and pepper to taste
1 cup of grated tomatoes

Select very red tomatoes, peel and grate, beginning at the blossom end. Make the mayonnaise and mix the two. This gives a custard-like mixture; freeze as you would ice cream. Serve over heart lettuce or a cucumber aspic. It should be seasoned well with red pepper and salt.

Burr Artichokes

Wash well, and let stand in salt water for 30 minutes or longer; this will draw out any insects or bugs. Drop into boiling water and cook about 30 minutes or until tender; pierce with a fork. Lift out, drain; place on a small dish and serve hot or cold with drawn butter, or a French dressing.

The dressing should be in a small dish so the leaves may be dipped into the dressing as each one is pulled off and eaten.

The tough part is thrown away, and the tender end eaten with the dressing. The good part is at the root of each leaf.

These artichokes sell for something like 12 to 15 cents each, though in some cities they are 5 cents each.

To eat a whole artichoke, steady it lightly with the fingers of the left hand, pull the leaves off one at a time with the thumb and a finger of the right hand, dip the thick white end into the butter or sauce and gently pull it between the teeth, thus removing the delicate meat held in this end. When all leaves are removed, the bottom or choke is cut and carried to the mouth with a fork.

An artichoke may be served as an entree with a sandwich or cracker, or as a salad with French dressing, having it hot or cold.

Burr Artichoke Bottoms or Chokes

This part of the burr artichoke may be purchased in cans, and is used generally for a cocktail.

Mock Chokes

Cut slices of small white turnips ¾ inch thick. Cover with cold water and bring slowly to boiling point. Drain and drop into a French dressing highly seasoned. Add enough water to cover and simmer until they can be pierced with a straw. Serve hot with melted butter or chill and serve as a cocktail with plenty of cocktail sauce.

Jerusalem Artichokes

These artichokes are commonly grown throughout the South in old fields, fence corners and gardens. They belong to the sunflower family. They are used generally for pickles and may be used as cucumbers peeled, sliced and served with vinegar, salt and pepper. They are very good cooked, but have been used this way very little.

Jerusalem Artichokes Cooked

Scrape and drop in cold water to prevent turning dark. Cut crosswise in half inch slices, and boil in salt water until just tender enough to be pierced with a fork. Drain and serve with melted butter or white sauce.

If overcooked, they are not crisp and tasty, but stringy.

Boiled Onions

Select onions of uniform size, peel, removing tops; let stand in cold water until ready to cook. Drain and cover with boiling salt water and cook gently, uncovered, until tender. Drain, return to the stew pan and dry slightly over a slow fire. Pour into a hot dish, cover with white sauce or melted butter, serve piping hot.

Fried Onions

Peel and slice in half-inch slices, crosswise.

Put into a saucepan, cover with boiling salt water, simmer for ten minutes, drain well. Into a fry pan place two tablespoons of butter or cooking oil or bacon drippings for every cup of onions. When hot add onions and fry until done tender and a delicate brown.

Stir frequently to prevent burning. Season with pepper and more salt if needed. Serve with steak or liver.

French Fried Onions

Cut onions in ¼-inch slices and pull ring loose. Soak in sweet milk for an hour (water may be used). Take rings from milk and cover with flour to which salt and pepper has been added; drop in deep fat and fry until brown. They should float in the grease.

They will go to the bottom at first, then come to top as they begin to get done. Don't fry too many at one time. A small batch often may be done quicker than too many at one time.

A kitchen stunt: Put flour in a paper bag, drop a handfull of onion rings in, shake well, and they are covered with flour. A thin batter of flour, sweet milk and egg with salt and pepper is sometimes used. However, the first is very simple.

Fried Onion Rings

Peel, slice into quarter-inch slices as many onions as needed. Have a vessel of deep fat, when hot drop in a handful and fry a delicate brown, remove, drain, sprinkle with salt, fry slowly enough to cook done. Do not fry too many at one time; a small quantity often will finish the job in less time and have better results.

If liked crisp, fry longer. These may garnish a broiled steak or any meat, or be served as a dish.

If you wish these onions very mild, soak for 1 hour in sweet milk, drain well, dredge with flour and fry as directed above.

Scalloped Onions No. 1

3 cups cooked onions
2 cups oyster crackers
½ cup buttered crumbs
¾ cup sweet milk

2 eggs
3 tablespoons butter
Salt and pepper to taste

Slice or quarter onions. Boil until done. Into a baking dish put a layer of onions, butter, salt, pepper. A layer of broken crackers, more onions and crackers until all are used. Mix milk and eggs together, pour over the mixture, cover top with buttered crumbs, bake just long enough to set the milk and eggs and brown top about 20 minutes. Serve in the dish in which it was baked. Have milk heated just tepid.

Scalloped Onions No. 2

1 quart onions (medium size)
2 cups white sauce
1 cup buttered crumbs

2 cups crackers
1 tablespoon minced parsley
Salt and pepper to taste

Peel, quarter and boil onions in salt water until tender. Follow directions for other scalloped dishes. Sometimes a little pimento pepper gives flavor and color. Cheese might cover the top in place of the crumbs, or a little mixed in the dish gives variety.

Glazed Onions

6 medium size onions
½ cup boiling water
3 tablespoons butter

¼ cup brown sugar
1 teaspoon salt
⅛ teaspoon pepper

Place peeled onions in covered baking pan or dish. Pour boiling water, butter over onions. Sprinkle with salt and pepper. Cover with brown sugar and bake in moderate oven one hour. Remove cover from dish for the last fifteen minutes. If large onions are used they may be quartered.

Onions as a Relish

Remove tops and outside peel. Drop into cold water until crisp and tender. Drain; eat with salt.

A spring salad would be to slice and mix with cucumbers and tomatoes. Serve with salt, vinegar and pepper or a French dressing.

A Southern Dish

1 quart peeled and diced shallots
6 eggs

¼ cup butter
Salt and pepper to taste

Boil shallots until done in salt water. Drain.

Into a fry pan put butter and melt gently. Add shallots and the eggs, which are broken but not beaten.

Stir gently as they cook to mix. Have a slow heat so the eggs will be tender. Cook the same as in scrambling eggs, and do not have them dry, but a soft creamy mixture; season, serve very hot. A bit of milk may be added. Any leftover meat, ham, or bacon, may be minced and added. This is a nice luncheon dish.

Onions au Gratin

Boil Spanish onions until done. Cut each onion in quarters. Put into baking dish a layer each of onions, white sauce, a sprinkle of grated cheese, crushed crackers, and repeat until dish is full. Cover top with buttered crumbs and slip in oven to brown on top and heat through. Serve in same dish.

To Cook Turnips

Peel and slice or dice the turnips. Just cover with boiling water. Add salt and a bit of sugar, boil until tender, about 20 or 30 minutes, drain and serve with white sauce or melted butter and chopped parsley. The white turnip and rutabagas are both good cooked this way, and make a pretty dish when mixed together.

Molded Turnips

2 cups of cooked and mashed turnips
1 cup of thick white sauce

3 eggs
Salt and pepper to taste

Cook, mash and put the turnips through a coarse strainer. Make the usual white sauce with milk, butter and flour. Mix the two together and add the eggs which have been beaten together just enough to break them well. Add salt and pepper. Pour the mixture into a buttered mold and set into a pan to cook in which several thicknesses of brown paper are put in the bottom. Pour boiling water to come half the depth of mold, bake or steam until firm. Unmold, garnish with parsley and serve hot.

Turnips and Pork

Peel, wash and slice turnips needed; then drop in cold water. Into a pot put a pork hock and let boil until done. Remove, add turnips and boil until tender. Drain, mash, season with more salt if necessary and add one tablespoon sugar. Serve with a small piece of pork and cornbread.

Sometimes a few Irish potatoes are cooked and mashed with turnips. This gives a more delicate flavor.

Turnips are much better cooked quickly; this keeps them from turning pink.

Rutabaga Turnip

This is a deep yellow turnip and requires much longer cooking than the white turnip, and is not so delicate. It may be boiled with a piece of pork, seasoning meat or served with melted butter or with sauce.

Carrots

Scrape or peel off outer skin and put into cold water until ready to cook. Boil moderately in salt water until tender, season with melted butter or white sauce. A little sugar added to the water is quite an improvement.

Uses

Carrots grated or diced, raw or cooked, may be used for salad.

Young, tender carrots are eaten raw the same as radishes.

Young, tender carrots with two or more tiny leaves left on are used for garnishes.

Carrots and beets, cooked separately and mixed and seasoned, may be used very effectively in carrying out a color scheme. Carrots and turnips may be used in the same way. (See recipe).

Carrots and Turnips

2 cups peeled and diced carrots   2 cups peeled and diced white turnips

Boil carrots and turnips separately until tender in salt water to which a little sugar has been added. Drain, mix together, season with melted butter or white sauce.

Carrots and Onions

Substitute onions for turnips. Follow recipe above.

Carrots and Peas

Use the first recipe and substitute peas for turnips, using half the quantity.

Carrot Mold

2 cups grated or shredded carrot   1 teaspoon salt
1 cup thick white sauce   Pepper to taste
3 eggs

Grate the carrots and put mixture in cheesecloth and press out some of the water; then measure. Make the usual white sauce. Half milk and half of the juice of the carrots may be used for the sauce. Add sauce to carrots, add seasoning, beat eggs together and add to mixture. Pour in a well-buttered ring mold and steam in hot water until firm, about 30 minutes. Let cool a few minutes, then unmold on platter and serve.

Parsnips and Salsify

The above are prepared, cooked and used similar to carrots.

Beets

Beets (roots) must be put into boiling water, cooked until tender (boil moderately) the time depends on the size and age of beets, from one to two hours. Do not trim off root nor cut leaves too close; if cut they bleed and lose their color.

Beets are sliced or diced and served hot with melted butter.

Beets as a Relish

Boil beets, slice or dice. Cover with a mild vinegar to which has been added a little salt and sugar.

Boiled Potatoes

Peel potatoes, remove any eyes or dark spots and put in cold water until ready to cook.

Drop into boiling water and boil rapidly for five or ten minutes, then reduce to medium heat and boil until done. Add salt when half done. Drain and place vessel over gentle fire; shake several times to turn potatoes to dry them out well, having pot uncovered. When dry, white and snowy looking, put into hot uncovered dish, dot with butter and serve at once. Potatoes may be peeled or boiled in their jackets.

Baked Potatoes

Select smooth, medium-sized potatoes, scrub well and with a fork stick several times (this prevents their bursting). Place in baking pan or on a rack (about center) in oven; bake forty-five minutes to one hour, according to size of potato. Have oven hot and reduce to medium.

To test, do not stick, but with a towel mash to see if soft. If done, continue to mash gently, but not hard enough to burst, until quite soft.

With a knife make a cross cut on each, about an inch and a half long, press hard to open. This sends out steam and meals the potato. Sprinkle with salt and paprika, add a lump of butter and place potatoes in platter on which is a folded napkin. If potatoes must wait, mash, open, and keep in warm oven until served. If potatoes are baked in too hot an oven the skins are heavy and hard and potatoes are not so good.

Stuffed Potatoes

Select medium-sized potatoes, prepare and bake as directed for baked potatoes. Remove a slice from one side, scoop out the inside, mash, season and refill shells, leaving the top of filling rough, place in a pan and into hot oven to reheat and brown the top. Serve very hot. The seasoning is usually milk and butter; a bit of cheese added is good, also minced bacon and onion.

Potato Puff

2 cups of hot mashed potatoes	2 tablespoons butter
1 cup milk more or less	2 teaspoons salt
1 egg	Sprinkle red pepper

Cook, dry and mash potatoes. Add milk and seasoning and beat well. Beat egg light, add to mixture and pile in a baking dish roughly. Bake in moderate oven about ten minutes. Serve immediately.

More eggs (two) would make a richer dish. If whites are beaten stiff and added the mixture will be lighter but will sometimes fall. A little grated cheese gives a nice flavor.

CHAPTER IV

Salads

While salads have been known and used for hundreds of years, yet it has remained for the last generation to recognize the value and importance of salads in our daily diet. A new adage says, "A salad a day keeps the doctor away." Salads, especially the raw varieties, contain mineral salts and vitamins which are so essential to our growth and general well being. Dietitians are advising families to reduce the quantity of other foods, especially the starches, and to increase the daily consumption of salads for every member of the household.

There is a general impression that salads are expensive and should be regarded as luxuries, but this is a mistake, since a little judicious planning will produce delicious and appetizing dishes of salads made wholly or in part of leftovers attractively arranged on lettuce leaves. The cost of the salad may be what you choose to make it, since coleslaw can be served in winter at about the cost of a dish of potatoes, and raw tomatoes in season at the cost of a dish of string beans. A sweet salad may take the place of a salad and dessert combined.

At the present time frozen and congealed fruit and vegetable salads are quite popular and certainly wholesome. It is far better to confine the meal to a few well selected balanced dishes than to too many. The mixtures are the cause of "lots" of indigestion.

The simple French dressing for salads for the hearty meal (salads should be light) is far more acceptable than mayonnaise, the latter being used where a heavy salad is used for the main dish. The secret of the perfect salad lies in the dressing and the plainest dinner may be made delightful by a well selected salad and dressing.

There is scarcely any limit to the many valuable crisp vegetables, fresh and canned fruits that are so plentiful. America takes the lead in producing the greatest variety of delicious vegetables and fruits, and is now the greatest salad eating nation. This is true of the better class; but since it is a known fact that the humble cabbage, carrots, lettuce and other commonly grown vegetables and fruits give so much food value, it is the desire of every one who is preparing food to stress salads. Salads may be put in the protective class of foods.

FRUIT SALADS

Pear Salad

Use canned pears; take from the can and let stand one hour in a good lemon water. Place on crisp lettuce two halves, make five or six balls from cottage or Neufchatel cheese, roll in chopped nut meats or chopped parsley, place on and around the pears, cover with French dressing and serve.

Porcupine Salad

Select large Bartlett pears, one for each serving. Have ready almonds, blanched and shredded lengthwise. Place pear on lettuce, with cut side down, stick almond pieces in rows like quills, put two cloves in small end for eyes. Serve with French dressing.

Apple Ring Salad

Core and slice into rings without peeling, bright red apples, ring ¼ inch thick, drop into salt water to keep white. When ready to use, dry and cover with French dressing. Core and remove seed and veins from crisp green peppers, cut in very thin rings. Arrange apple and pepper rings on crisp lettuce, garnish with pimentoes. Serve with French dressing.

Waldorf Salad

1 quart peeled and diced apple	1 pint chopped blanched almonds
1 quart chopped celery	1 cup mayonnaise

Blanch and chop the nuts, cut celery and sprinkle with salt; put where both will keep cool. Make mayonnaise. Peel and dice apples one at a time and mix with the mayonnaise until you have a quart. When ready to serve mix in the nuts and celery; add more seasoning if needed; drain the celery free from any water; put into apples or on lettuce and serve. When apples are cut and mixed at once with the mayonnaise they will not turn dark. Any nuts may be used. The almonds are white and pretty.

Log Cabin Salad

Peel and cut bananas in fourths lengthwise, soak in orange juice one hour. Arrange on lettuce log cabin style, fill center with any fruit desired, cherries, pineapple, grapefruit. Serve with mayonnaise or French dressing.
The bananas may be rolled in chopped nuts before piling, if liked.

Pineapple and Cheese Salad

½ cup cottage cheese (or two Neufchatel cheese)	4 slices canned pineapple
	½ teaspoon paprika
2 or 3 tablespoons top milk or sweet cream (more or less)	Pinch of salt
	Dash of cayenne

Mash cheese and soften into firm paste, using sufficient milk or cream, and add seasoning. Wipe slices of pineapple dry, so cheese will stick to fruit. Put layer of cheese as deep as the pineapple, then another slice of pineapple, press together hard, let stand with a weight on top until cold. Cut in small pie shaped sections, pile on crisp lettuce. Serve with pineapple dressing. See recipe. This is a nice sweet salad.

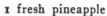

Pineapple and Cheese Salad

1 fresh pineapple	1 cup whipped cream
¼ pound of rich soft cream cheese	1 head lettuce
1 cup mayonnaise	Salt and cayenne pepper to season

Peel and remove the eyes of the pineapple. From the stem end pluck off the pineapple in nice size cubes, going round and round the stem until all is removed. Moisten the cheese with a bit of milk, if necessary, and make into balls about as large as a marble. Wash and have lettuce crisp. Pile pineapple and cheese balls on the lettuce. Mix the cream with the mayonnaise and put a generous spoonful over top. Serve at once after the dressing has been added. This will make eight or ten portions.

Butterfly Salad

The arrangement of this salad in the form of a butterfly is not a new one, but the fruit mixture is a good one. Including raw apple in fruit salads not only improves the flavor, but makes the more expensive fruits go further.

2 slices canned pineapple	Strips of pimento
2 slices orange	Lettuce
2 slices unpared apples	Chopped nuts
½ pound Malaga grapes	

Cut the pineapple slices in half and place the round edges together on the plate. Over this fit the slices of apple with the core removed. (If you wish to remove the skin pour boiling water on the apple and the skin will peel off, leaving the red coloring showing in the meat). On top of this fit the orange slices, which have been allowed to stand in sugar at least 20 minutes. Form the butterfly's body from the grapes and the antennae from the pimento strips. Sprinkle with nut meats and serve with mayonnaise.

Stuffed Cherry and Pineapple Salad

1 cup white canned cherries	1 cup diced pineapple
½ cup blanched almonds	

Drain fruit, dice pineapple, remove seed from cherries and into each one stick an almond. Pile together on crisp lettuce and serve with fruit salad dressing. Plain mayonnaise may be used, or mayonnaise with whipped cream.

Peach Salad

Select 8 halves of firm peaches	1 cup whipped cream (more or less)
2 Neufchatel cheese (about ½ cup)	¼ cup French dressing
½ cup nut meats or salted peanuts	

Place a half of peach on crisp lettuce. Make cheese into balls and fill centers of peaches. Mix French dressing into cream, which should be quite stiff. Add more seasoning if necessary. Put portion on top of cheese, add peach, sprinkle with nuts and serve.

Mary Louise Salad

Peel grapefruit and remove sections whole, allowing 5 or 6 sections for each person. Have crisp lettuce and arrange grapefruit in shape of cart

wheel. Fill center with chopped pecan meats and seeded cherries or Malaga grapes and serve wih French dressing, using the juice of the grapefruit in place of lemon. Have everything cold when served.

Bessie Tift College Salad

2 cups diced apples
1 cup cherries (red or white)
1 cup diced pineapple

1 cup nut meats
1 dozen mint leaves, chopped very fine

Seed cherries, dice all fruit, mixing the first three, and add mint leaves. Arrange on lettuce, cover with dressing, sprinkle nut meats over top and serve.

For the dressing use:

⅔ cup sugar
½ cup water

2 eggs
3 tablespoons lemon or grapefruit juice

Boil sugar and water until it threads well, pour over the stiff beaten whites, as in making icing. Beat yolks light, add to mixture, place bowl over boiling water and cook (beating all the time) until thick. Remove from fire, add lemon juice, beat until cold. Serve over fruit salad.

Southern Salad

2 cups diced tart apples, unpeeled
3 bananas, peeled and diced
Meat of 1 large grapefruit

1 cup white grapes, peeled and seeded
Season with salt and cayenne pepper

Mix all together and serve on lettuce, using a whipped cream dressing.

Grapefruit Salad

Peel and remove sections of grapefruit, keeping sections intact, place five sections on a crisp lettuce leaf in melon shape. Have Neufchatel cheese softened to a stiff paste with a bit of milk, put into a forcing bag with star end pastry tube and make four or five roses around the grapefruit. Over all put French dressing and serve. This is a nice dinner salad.

College Salad

1 can pineapple, cut in cubes

Equal quantity marshmallow, cut small

Make a fruit dressing (see recipe). Using about one cup, put this over the pineapple and marshmallow to stand about two hours. When ready to serve, add a cup of pecan meats, or any nut preferred. Add more dressing, if necessary. Serve on lettuce.

Avocado Salad (Alligator Pear) No. 1

Select medium sized, firm avocados, chill, cut in half, remove seed. Make a French dressing and put a portion into the pear, place on plate and serve with crackers or sandwich. Grated onion added to the dressing is much liked by many. Russian or Thousand Island dressing is used also.

If the avocado is to be used with other ingredients, peel, remove the seed and cut into sections or cubes.

Avocado Salad No. 2

Select ripe avocado, peel, cut and mash to a pulp, season with lemon juice, salt and pepper, make into small balls about the size of bird egg, roll in very finely chopped green pepper. Have crisp lettuce ready, on this place one thick slice of ripe tomato and five balls, leaving space in center to make a rosette of mayonnaise. Serve.

Santiago Salad

Peel and cut in cubes as much avocado as needed, mix a small onion, grated, salt and lime or lemon juice, mix with avocado, pile on lettuce on platter. Over all sprinkle finely chopped hard boiled eggs. Use more dressing if desired. The eggs may be rubbed through a coarse strainer, which gives a pretty effect.

Avocado Nut Salad

Mix two parts diced avocado to one part nut meats. Place on crisp ettuce and serve with any preferred dressing.

Avocado Aspic

2 cups water
¼ cup lemon juice
1 good sized avocado
2 large firm tomatoes
2 tablespoons sugar
1 teaspoon salt

½ box Knox No. 1 gelatine (1 envelope) in ¼ cup cold water
1 tablespoon grated onion, if desired
Cayenne and paprika to taste
Green coloring to make green

Put gelatine to soak for five minutes, then melt over hot water. Peel and dice avocado and tomato. Make a stock of the water and seasoning, add coloring and melted gelatine. Into a mold put a portion of stock, set on ice, put in a layer of fruit when beginning to get firm, then more stock and more fruit until all is used. Place on ice to get hard, unmold on lettuce, serve with mayonnaise.

An easy way is to pour all the stock into mold, and when it begins to get firm, drop in the fruit, stir gently to mix, let get firm.

Avocado and Tomato

Peel ripe, firm tomatoes, cut into sections lengthwise, peel and cut avocado same way, alternate the sections red and green on crisp lettuce leaf, serve with French dressing.

Avocado and Egg Salad

If they are of the small Mexican variety, peel and mash avocados, one for each guest. The American avocado is larger, and one will serve two guests. Chop or mince 1 hard-boiled egg, mince 1 small onion, add vinegar, salt and pepper to taste. Serve on a lettuce leaf. This also makes a delicious sandwich filling.

Stuffed Lettuce

Have crisp hearts of lettuce, and after removing any coarse outside leaves, cut them in halves crosswise and remove a little of the center. The halved hearts will then have the appearance of nests. Make some small eggs from cream cheese, sprinkle with black pepper and paprika, and put five or six in each nest. Put a large spoonful of red jelly over each portion and serve with French dressing, seasoned with paprika.

Head Lettuce with Roquefort Cheese Dressing

Make a French dressing, mash cheese until fine, add small portion of dressing to soften, continue until well mixed. Cut firm lettuce in quarters, put about two tablespoons of dressing over lettuce, serve.

Okra Salad

Select small tender pods of okra about 2½ inches long. Allow about six pods to each serving. Do not cut off point, and trim stem end like a pencil point. Boil until tender in salted water to which is added a little vinegar and one teaspoon of paprika. When tender drain and chill. Serve with French dressing. Arrange okra pods on lettuce leaf with stem ends at center and each pod extending out like spokes in a wheel. Put radish rose or sprig of parsley in center.

Tomato Salad

Select ripe and well shaped tomatoes and peel. Across the blossom end of tomato cut half way through into eight sections, pull open like a lily, leaving tomato intact at stem end. Serve with mayonnaise, cucumber mayonnaise, or French dressing.

Another Stuffed Tomato

Prepare tomatoes as in above recipe. Use tomatoes and fresh or canned pineapple to fill centers, using French dressing for filling and topping with mayonnaise.

Novelty Salad

6 hard boiled eggs	1 cup finely chopped chicken
1 tablespoon each, finely chopped green peppers and pimentoes	Sufficient mayonnaise to mix Salt and pepper to taste

Cut eggs lengthwise, remove yolks and rub through sieve. Toss all ingredients together, add seasoning and enough mayonnaise to hold together, refill egg whites, arrange on crisp lettuce, serve with mayonnaise. Each egg may be placed on thick slice of tomato then on lettuce. Garnish with strips of pimentoes, celery, celery hearts or any other garnish.

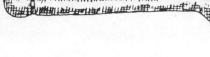

Vegetable Combination Salad

1 slice tomato (half inch thick)	2 rings green pepper
2 rings onion (Bermuda is best)	2 stalks asparagus

Place on lettuce leaf, serve with French dressing. Over all sprinkle beets cut in small pieces.

Another Vegetable Salad

Cooked beets, sliced or diced	Chopped olives
Cooked carrots, sliced or diced	English peas
Chopped celery	Proportions to suit individual

Mix all together and serve on lettuce with French dressing.

Creole Salad

4 cups macaroni cooked (about ½ lb. raw)	¼ cup sliced stuffed olives
2 cups diced tomatoes	2 tablespoons grated onion
1 cup grated cheese	½ clove garlic chopped fine
1 cup mayonnaise	⅛ teaspoon cayenne pepper

Boil macaroni in salt water until tender, but not mushy, blanch (wash well in cold water), drain, cut in inch pieces and place on cheesecloth to drain and chill. Have very cold. Measure after cooked. Mix all together as any salad and serve on lettuce.

This is a good salad for Dutch Supper, served with dill pickles and rye bread.

Miss Evelyn's Spanish Salad

1 dozen hard-tack or ship biscuit	3 tender cucumbers
4 large ripe tomatoes (more if necessary)	4 canned pimentoes
	1 cup mayonnaise

Put hard-tack in cold water until soft. Drain, and through a potato ricer or colander, mash the hard-tack. This should look like potatoes when riced. Into a bowl put a layer of the riced biscuit, then a layer of the tomatoes, sliced very thin, a layer of mayonnaise, another layer of riced hard-tack, a layer of cucumbers, sliced very thin, a layer of mayonnaise; next comes hard-tack, pimentoes, minced, and mayonnaise. Over the top a layer of riced hard-tack, and over this place slices of tomatoes cut in fancy shapes. Place all in ice box until thoroughly chilled and seasoned. Serve from the bowl. A bit of grated onion may be added, or rub the bowl with a clove of garlic cut in half. The mayonnaise should be highly seasoned.

Stuffed Celery

Select uniform pieces of celery, leaving the pretty leaves on; mash sufficient cottage, Neufchatel or cream cheese, soften with top milk, season with salt and cayenne pepper. Fill centers of celery with mixture, roll in chopped nuts, place on ice to keep cold and crisp. Serve as a salad or to accompany a salad.

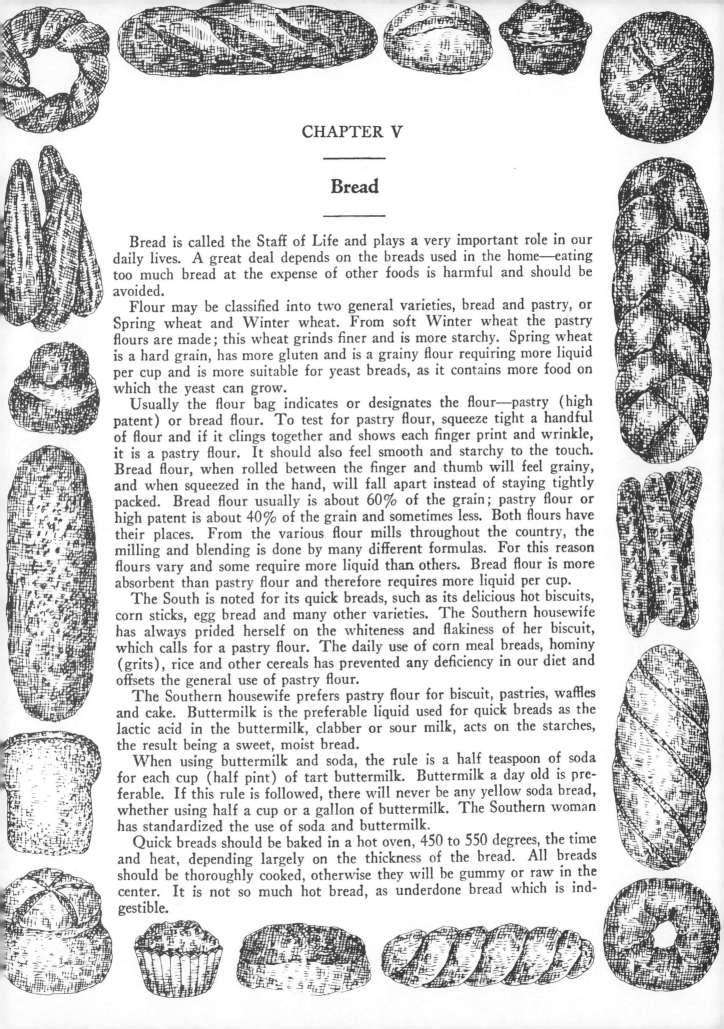

CHAPTER V

Bread

Bread is called the Staff of Life and plays a very important role in our daily lives. A great deal depends on the breads used in the home—eating too much bread at the expense of other foods is harmful and should be avoided.

Flour may be classified into two general varieties, bread and pastry, or Spring wheat and Winter wheat. From soft Winter wheat the pastry flours are made; this wheat grinds finer and is more starchy. Spring wheat is a hard grain, has more gluten and is a grainy flour requiring more liquid per cup and is more suitable for yeast breads, as it contains more food on which the yeast can grow.

Usually the flour bag indicates or designates the flour—pastry (high patent) or bread flour. To test for pastry flour, squeeze tight a handful of flour and if it clings together and shows each finger print and wrinkle, it is a pastry flour. It should also feel smooth and starchy to the touch. Bread flour, when rolled between the finger and thumb will feel grainy, and when squeezed in the hand, will fall apart instead of staying tightly packed. Bread flour usually is about 60% of the grain; pastry flour or high patent is about 40% of the grain and sometimes less. Both flours have their places. From the various flour mills throughout the country, the milling and blending is done by many different formulas. For this reason flours vary and some require more liquid than others. Bread flour is more absorbent than pastry flour and therefore requires more liquid per cup.

The South is noted for its quick breads, such as its delicious hot biscuits, corn sticks, egg bread and many other varieties. The Southern housewife has always prided herself on the whiteness and flakiness of her biscuit, which calls for a pastry flour. The daily use of corn meal breads, hominy (grits), rice and other cereals has prevented any deficiency in our diet and offsets the general use of pastry flour.

The Southern housewife prefers pastry flour for biscuit, pastries, waffles and cake. Buttermilk is the preferable liquid used for quick breads as the lactic acid in the buttermilk, clabber or sour milk, acts on the starches, the result being a sweet, moist bread.

When using buttermilk and soda, the rule is a half teaspoon of soda for each cup (half pint) of tart buttermilk. Buttermilk a day old is preferable. If this rule is followed, there will never be any yellow soda bread, whether using half a cup or a gallon of buttermilk. The Southern woman has standardized the use of soda and buttermilk.

Quick breads should be baked in a hot oven, 450 to 550 degrees, the time and heat, depending largely on the thickness of the bread. All breads should be thoroughly cooked, otherwise they will be gummy or raw in the center. It is not so much hot bread, as underdone bread which is indgestible.

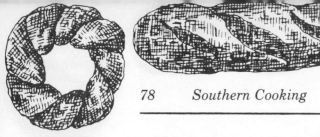

There are many who prefer sweet milk and baking powder. The standard measurement of baking powder, when using sweet milk, is two teaspoons for each cup of flour. In many of her breads, however, the Southern housewife prefers buttermilk with soda and a small quantity of baking powder, which gives a light fluffy result, lessening labor (beating) and the number of eggs.

QUICK BREADS

Buttermilk Biscuit

2 cups flour (2½ after sifted)   1 teaspoon salt
1 cup buttermilk   ½ teaspoon soda
4 tablespoons shortening

Into the flour put salt, soda, and sift into bowl. Mix in shortening with tips of fingers, or chop in with spoon, add buttermilk, using spoon, and make into a dough. Lift onto a well floured board, knead just to get smooth and firm enough to handle. Roll or pat out to one-half inch thick, cut, place on baking sheet, bake in hot oven about ten minutes. Acid buttermilk is better for cooking, and for every cup of milk one-half teaspoon soda is necessary. Use a tea biscuit cutter.

Drop Biscuit

1 pint flour   ½ teaspoon soda
1 teaspoon salt   4 tablespoons shortening (lard)
2 teaspoons baking powder   1 cup buttermilk

Sift flour into which is put the salt, soda and baking powder, into a mixing bowl. Mix in the shortening with tips of fingers or chop in with spoon.

Mix into a dough with the buttermilk. Stir and mix well, but quickly. Drop with a spoon, pieces about as large as a walnut, leaving space between. Bake in quick oven about 10 minutes or until done.

20th Century Buttermilk Biscuit

Use recipe for Buttermilk Biscuit, add two teaspoons baking powder to flour. Follow first recipe exactly. Either white or brown flour may be used with any of these recipes.

Baking Powder Biscuit No. 1

2 cups flour   4 teaspoons baking powder
1 cup sweet milk (more or less)   1 teaspoon salt
4 tablespoons shortening

Sift dry ingredients with flour, mix in shortening, add sweet milk and make into a dough, knead slightly, roll, cut and bake. Do not crowd in pan.

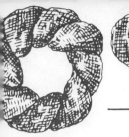

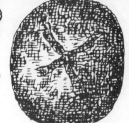

Baking Powder Biscuit No. 2

Use first recipe, add 1 teaspoon sugar. Follow directions, making a firm dough. Knead until smooth and rather stiff, using extra flour if necessary. Roll out one-fourth inch thick and cut with small size cutter with stickers in center, or stick several times with fork. Place on baking sheet, leaving space so sides will brown. Bake in quick oven until a pretty brown. The tops may be brushed with sweet milk when nearly done if a glaze is wanted.

Scotch Scones

2 cups flour (sifted before measuring)	3 teaspoons baking powder
	¼ cup butter
⅓ cup sugar	2 eggs
¼ teaspoon salt	½ cup milk, or more if needed

Sift baking powder, salt and sugar with flour. Chop in the butter as in making pastry. Beat eggs together, add the milk and mix with the flour making a soft dough using a little more flour if necessary to handle. Lift to a well floured board, knead lightly, roll out to ¼ inch thick. Cut, using a large biscuit cutter. Place on moderately hot griddle and bake as a hoe cake, turning when well brown. Cook slowly for thorough cooking. Serve immediately with butter and jam. Any scones left over may be split, toasted and served hot. This is something like English muffins.

Party Biscuit

2½ cups flour	4 teaspoons baking powder
⅓ cup shortening	1 teaspoon salt
¾ cup milk	1 tablespoon sugar
1 egg	

Sift sugar, salt and baking powder with flour. Break egg in cup and mix well; fill with sweet milk. Mix shortening into flour, mix into dough with milk and egg, using spoon. Turn onto a well floured board and knead until smooth, using extra flour if necessary. Roll out to one-fourth inch thick, cut with tea biscuit cutter, butter one-half, turn over (like Parker House rolls), place on baking sheet and bake in quick oven until done (10 to 12 minutes).

Raisin Biscuit

Use recipe for Party Biscuit. Add 1 cup seedless raisins, knead until smooth, cut and bake.

These may be turned or left round. If round, roll dough half inch thick before cutting.

Miss Mary's Beaten Biscuit

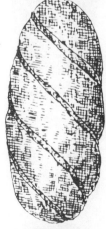

4 cups flour (sifted)	1 teaspoon salt
¾ cup milk (more or less)	1 teaspoon sugar
⅓ cup lard	

Sift sugar and salt into flour, mix in shortening and make a very stiff

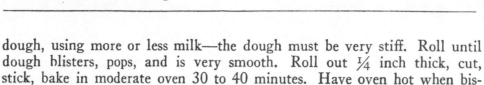

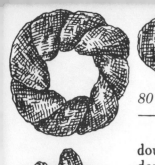

dough, using more or less milk—the dough must be very stiff. Roll until dough blisters, pops, and is very smooth. Roll out ¼ inch thick, cut, stick, bake in moderate oven 30 to 40 minutes. Have oven hot when biscuits are put into same.

Mrs. M's Beaten Biscuit

6 cups flour (sifted)	2 teaspoons sugar
¾ cup lard	2 teaspoons salt
½ cup ice water	

Dissolve sugar and salt in water. Sift flour four times. Mix in lard thoroughly and water little at a time, never getting any portion of flour very wet. The dough must be very stiff. Roll twenty minutes or until it blisters and pops.

Put into hot oven for few minutes then reduce heat and bake about 40 minutes at medium heat, about 350 degrees.

Georgia Beaten Biscuit

1 quart pastry flour	1 cup of sweet milk, ice cold, more
6 tablespoons of lard	or less, to make a stiff dough
1 teaspoon salt	

Sift salt into the flour, mix in the lard, add the sweet milk, being very careful to have the dough very stiff, even if you leave out some of the milk. Beat or grind in biscuit break for 20 minutes. Cut one-half inch thick with a small cutter made for beaten biscuit with stickers in center (or stick with a fork), bake in slow oven 20 to 40 minutes until brown and crisp.

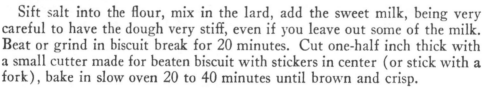
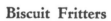

Biscuit Fritters

Use recipe for biscuit made with sweet milk. Roll out dough thin, cut with large cutter, place spoonful of jam or stewed fruit on one-half wet edge, cover with other half, press together with fork or fingers, fry in deep fat, drain, sprinkle with powdered sugar.

Sweet Potato Biscuit

To 20th Century biscuit recipe add 1 cup of mashed and strained sweet potatoes (hot or cold). 1 tablespoon of sugar, using more or less milk as necessary, have dough firm. Cut, bake in hot oven. Less shortening may be used. An egg may be added.

Porter Puffs
(5 o'Clock Tea Puffs)

4 tablespoons butter	6 teaspoons baking powder
1 egg	½ teaspoon salt
1 cup sweet milk	Sufficient flour to make a stiff
2 tablespoons sugar	batter

Beat egg together very lightly, add milk and all ingredients, add melted butter last.

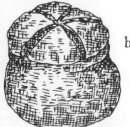

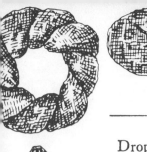

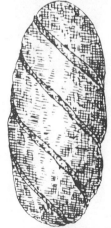

Drop a teaspoonful into well greased muffin tins, sizzling hot, bake in hot oven. Have some butter melted and in a small pitcher. Puncture side of muffin with pitcher, pour in about a teaspoon of melted butter and serve at once.

Quick Sally Lunn

½ cup butter, or shortening
½ cup sugar
2 cups flour, sifted then measured
1 cup milk
¾ teaspoon salt
4 teaspoons baking powder
3 eggs

Cream shortening and sugar together well, add eggs one at a time quickly, but well. Sift salt and baking powder with flour. Alternately add milk and flour to egg mixture, mixing quickly with as little stirring as possible until free of lumps and smooth. Pour into deep layer cake pan, bake at 425 degrees for 30 minutes. Serve hot with butter. This may be baked in large muffin pans for individual Lunns.

Aunt Sweet's Quick Sally Lunn

2 eggs
¾ cup milk
2½ cups flour
3 tablespoons butter
2 tablespoons sugar
1 teaspoon salt
4 teaspoons baking powder

Beat eggs together until very light, add sugar, mix as in making cake, having baking powder and salt sifted with flour, add melted butter last. Drop in hot, greased muffin tins, or bake in round layer pans. Cut in pie shape sections, serve hot with butter. Use more or less flour to have batter as thick as muffin batter. Use hot oven.

Cheese Biscuit

Roll out biscuit dough to one-fourth inch thickness. Spread generously with grated cheese, sprinkle with red pepper, roll up like a jelly roll. Cut one-half inch or more across the roll, place on greased baking sheet and bake in moderate oven until done and brown. They are good hot or cold. Leave space for biscuit to spread.

Wheat Muffins

2 eggs
1 cup sweet milk
1½ cups flour
1 tablespoon oil
1 teaspoon sugar
1 teaspoon salt
3 teaspoons baking powder

Separate eggs, beat yolks light; add milk, oil, salt and sugar; now add flour; beat whites stiff; fold in; now mix in baking powder. Put into greased muffin tins; bake in hot oven, 15 to 20 minutes on top rack.

CORNMEAL BREADS OF VARIOUS KINDS

Cornmeal Muffins

2 eggs	2 teaspoons salt
2½ cups sifted meal	1 teaspoon soda
2 cups buttermilk	3 teaspoons baking powder
3 tablespoons melted shortening	

Beat eggs together until light. Add milk, shortening and salt.

Add meal, being careful in putting in, as meal varies and the batter should be a medium batter. Beat smooth. Grease and heat pans. Sift in the baking powder and dissolve the soda in a spoonful of cold water. Add to mixture, stir well and pour into molds. Bake in good hot oven until brown and crusty—about 15 to 20 minutes.

This same recipe can be used for corn sticks or egg-bread.

If the batter is too thin, the muffins will be sticky; if too stiff, dry and tough. No flour is used in corn sticks, muffins or egg-bread. The real Southern cornmeal is sufficiently fine to hold the bread together. The bran is sifted from the meal.

Corn Sticks

2 eggs	1 teaspoon sugar
2 cups sifted meal	2 teaspoons salt
2 cups buttermilk	1 teaspoon soda
3 tablespoons melted shortening	3 teaspoons baking powder

Beat eggs together until light. Add milk, shortening and salt.

Add meal, being careful in putting in, as meal varies and the batter should be a medium batter. Beat smooth. Grease and heat stick pans. Sift in the baking powder and dissolve the soda in a spoonful of cold water. Add to mixture, stir well and pour into molds. Bake in good hot oven until brown and crusty—about 15 to 20 minutes. Corn sticks need a batter some thinner than muffins.

Egg Bread

Make the same as cornmeal muffins. Pour into baking pan, well greased and piping hot, bake in hot oven about twenty to thirty minutes, according to thickness. Egg bread should be about one and one-half inches thick when done, with a good brown crust bottom and top. Cut in squares to serve. If baked in pan with sides too deep, the top does not brown well.

Cornmeal Hoecake

2 cups sifted meal	Cold water to mix
½ teaspoon salt	

Mix meal with water sufficient to handle, let stand a few minutes to see if more water is needed to spread. Have a heavy griddle greased and hot, pour on the mixture and pat out into a round cake, having about one-half inch thick; reduce fire and let brown, turn and brown other side. Cook altogether about thirty minutes. Serve hot with butter.

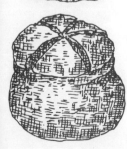

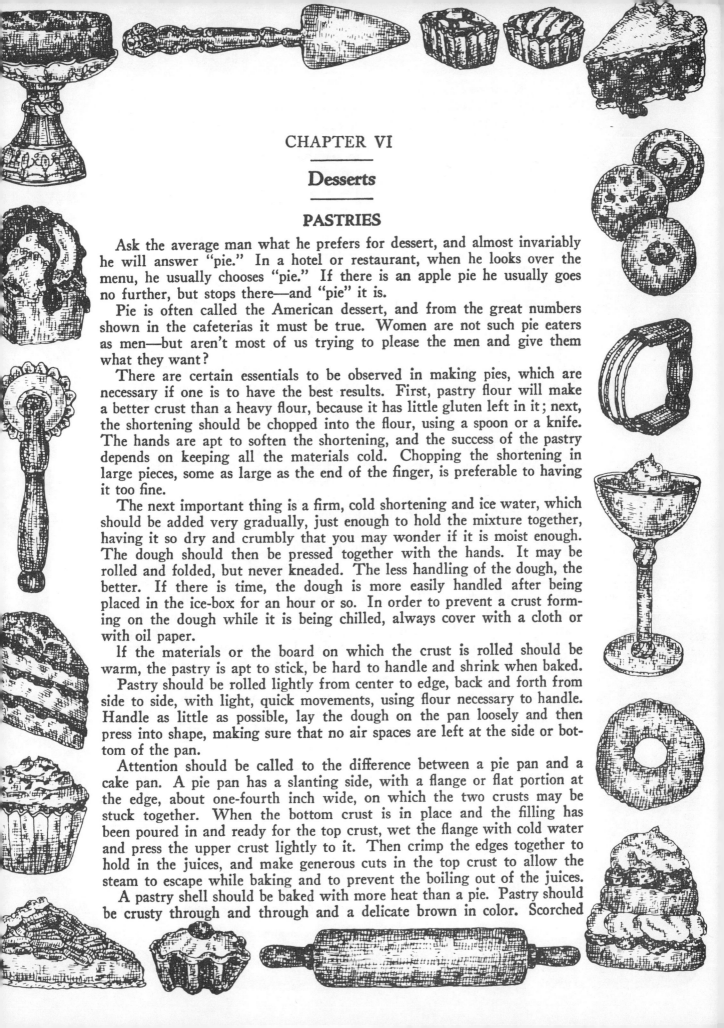

CHAPTER VI

Desserts

PASTRIES

Ask the average man what he prefers for dessert, and almost invariably he will answer "pie." In a hotel or restaurant, when he looks over the menu, he usually chooses "pie." If there is an apple pie he usually goes no further, but stops there—and "pie" it is.

Pie is often called the American dessert, and from the great numbers shown in the cafeterias it must be true. Women are not such pie eaters as men—but aren't most of us trying to please the men and give them what they want?

There are certain essentials to be observed in making pies, which are necessary if one is to have the best results. First, pastry flour will make a better crust than a heavy flour, because it has little gluten left in it; next, the shortening should be chopped into the flour, using a spoon or a knife. The hands are apt to soften the shortening, and the success of the pastry depends on keeping all the materials cold. Chopping the shortening in large pieces, some as large as the end of the finger, is preferable to having it too fine.

The next important thing is a firm, cold shortening and ice water, which should be added very gradually, just enough to hold the mixture together, having it so dry and crumbly that you may wonder if it is moist enough. The dough should then be pressed together with the hands. It may be rolled and folded, but never kneaded. The less handling of the dough, the better. If there is time, the dough is more easily handled after being placed in the ice-box for an hour or so. In order to prevent a crust forming on the dough while it is being chilled, always cover with a cloth or with oil paper.

If the materials or the board on which the crust is rolled should be warm, the pastry is apt to stick, be hard to handle and shrink when baked.

Pastry should be rolled lightly from center to edge, back and forth from side to side, with light, quick movements, using flour necessary to handle. Handle as little as possible, lay the dough on the pan loosely and then press into shape, making sure that no air spaces are left at the side or bottom of the pan.

Attention should be called to the difference between a pie pan and a cake pan. A pie pan has a slanting side, with a flange or flat portion at the edge, about one-fourth inch wide, on which the two crusts may be stuck together. When the bottom crust is in place and the filling has been poured in and ready for the top crust, wet the flange with cold water and press the upper crust lightly to it. Then crimp the edges together to hold in the juices, and make generous cuts in the top crust to allow the steam to escape while baking and to prevent the boiling out of the juices.

A pastry shell should be baked with more heat than a pie. Pastry should be crusty through and through and a delicate brown in color. Scorched

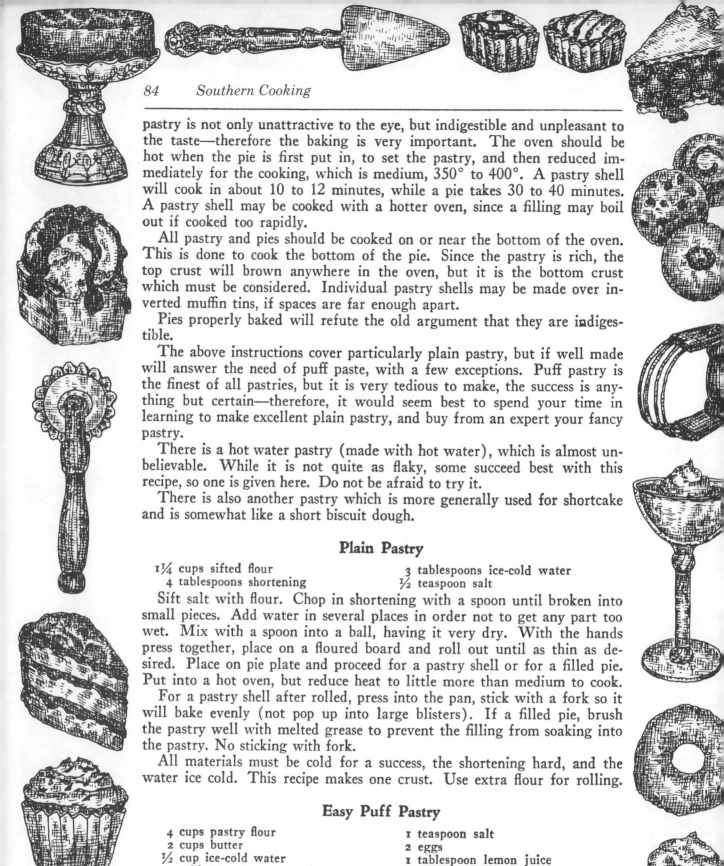

pastry is not only unattractive to the eye, but indigestible and unpleasant to the taste—therefore the baking is very important. The oven should be hot when the pie is first put in, to set the pastry, and then reduced immediately for the cooking, which is medium, 350° to 400°. A pastry shell will cook in about 10 to 12 minutes, while a pie takes 30 to 40 minutes. A pastry shell may be cooked with a hotter oven, since a filling may boil out if cooked too rapidly.

All pastry and pies should be cooked on or near the bottom of the oven. This is done to cook the bottom of the pie. Since the pastry is rich, the top crust will brown anywhere in the oven, but it is the bottom crust which must be considered. Individual pastry shells may be made over inverted muffin tins, if spaces are far enough apart.

Pies properly baked will refute the old argument that they are indigestible.

The above instructions cover particularly plain pastry, but if well made will answer the need of puff paste, with a few exceptions. Puff pastry is the finest of all pastries, but it is very tedious to make, the success is anything but certain—therefore, it would seem best to spend your time in learning to make excellent plain pastry, and buy from an expert your fancy pastry.

There is a hot water pastry (made with hot water), which is almost unbelievable. While it is not quite as flaky, some succeed best with this recipe, so one is given here. Do not be afraid to try it.

There is also another pastry which is more generally used for shortcake and is somewhat like a short biscuit dough.

Plain Pastry

1¼ cups sifted flour   3 tablespoons ice-cold water
4 tablespoons shortening   ½ teaspoon salt

Sift salt with flour. Chop in shortening with a spoon until broken into small pieces. Add water in several places in order not to get any part too wet. Mix with a spoon into a ball, having it very dry. With the hands press together, place on a floured board and roll out until as thin as desired. Place on pie plate and proceed for a pastry shell or for a filled pie. Put into a hot oven, but reduce heat to little more than medium to cook.

For a pastry shell after rolled, press into the pan, stick with a fork so it will bake evenly (not pop up into large blisters). If a filled pie, brush the pastry well with melted grease to prevent the filling from soaking into the pastry. No sticking with fork.

All materials must be cold for a success, the shortening hard, and the water ice cold. This recipe makes one crust. Use extra flour for rolling.

Easy Puff Pastry

4 cups pastry flour   1 teaspoon salt
2 cups butter   2 eggs
½ cup ice-cold water   1 tablespoon lemon juice
1 tablespoon sugar

Add salt and sugar to flour in mixing bowl; chop butter into flour as fine as possible, having butter very cold. Beat eggs together for five minutes, add lemon juice to them, add the cold water and mix flour into a stiff dough. Lift dough to well-floured board, roll out into rectangular shape, fold all four sides onto the dough, roll again; repeat this process four times. Fold again and wrap in a napkin, place on plate and stand on ice or let stand until thoroughly chilled. Roll out again and use for patties, pie crust or tart shells.

Never Fail Hot Water Pastry

2½ cups flour
½ cup boiling water
¼ teaspoon baking powder

1 teaspoon salt
½ cup shortening (half butter may be used)

Cream the shortening with the water by adding the latter only a little at a time. Mix the salt and baking powder with the sifted flour and stir this into the shortening and water. Turn out upon a floured board and roll thin. This amount will make upper and lower crusts for one large pie.

Pastry for Shortcake

2½ cups flour
⅔ cup firm cold shortening

6 tablespoons ice-cold water
2 teaspoons salt

Chop shortening into flour until it looks like meal. With a spoon mix into a very dry, stiff ball, using less liquid if necessary to have it very dry. With hands press into a ball; do not knead at all.

Lift on a well floured board, using extra flour to handle. Divide into two parts, roll out thin and bake two pastry shells. Fill the shells with strawberries, putting one on top of the other, like layer cake. Top with whipped cream.

When ready to bake crust, prick with a fork in many places to prevent blistering. Do not have pastry very brown, have a light color but crisp.

Individual Tart or Pie Shells

Roll and cut pastry with large cutter, or the desired size, stick with fork to prevent blistering, place carelessly over inverted patty pans or individual molds and bake as any pastry, a light brown but crusty. Fill with any desired filling, fruits or custards. Cover top with a soft icing, run under the blaze to brown quickly and serve hot or cold. Meringue may cover top.

Jelly glasses and empty spools may be used. Grease slightly before placing on pastry. Put molds on large baking sheet and many may be baked at once. Tiny shells filled with marmalade, topped with an icing, may be used as French pastry.

Paté or Patty Cases of Puff Pastry

To cut patties: Roll dough ¾-inch thick, use tea biscuit cutter. Make another cut and remove center. Wet first piece with cold water and place ring on top, press together well. Place carefully on baking sheet, not too close, chill before baking. Bake tops, which are the removed pieces from ring. Remove the inside, which is a soft dough which refuses to get crisp, fill and replace top. Never brown too much. Puff paste must be light brown, but crisp. This may be used for pie crust.

Use more or less of the liquid, according to what the flour requires. Use extra flour for rolling. Everything must be ice-cold.

Place in center of hot oven which registers 500 degrees, reduce heat 50 degrees every five minutes until thermometer reads 300 degrees. Continue cooking until a golden brown (about 30 to 40 minutes).

Several thicknesses of paper placed in bottom of pan will prevent cases from burning. A bright pan does not burn easily.

Timbales

Timbale cases are used to hold creamed dishes (meats or vegetables). Timbale cases and pastry patés are used for the same purpose; timbales hold the hot filling, while patés (or patties) and filling both must be hot.

Rosettes are another form of timbale, and may be sweet or plain. They are used for vegetables or fruit.

To Make Timbales

1 cup milk	1 egg
1 cup water	Flour to make a thin batter, about 2½
1 teaspoon salt	cups

Into a bowl put the milk, half the water, salt and egg unbeaten, beat enough to mix the egg into the milk using a stirring motion to get as little air as possible into the mixture.

Add flour and mix well until free of lumps. Add the remaining water, which gives a thin batter. Cover and let stand until the bubbles come to the top, an hour or more. Pour a portion into a small bowl large enough to float the timbale iron, dip into batter, let dry, then fry in hot grease until a light brown. Slip out the iron, fill the shell with the hot grease and continue cooking until crisp; remove with a fork; drain on paper. Keep the iron in the boiling fat while finishing the timbale and repeat the process.

Before dipping into the batter, wipe off the mold on a piece of soft paper before cooking each timbale. As the batter is used keep filled with the cold portion. It's better not to use the entire portion because the hot iron makes the batter too thin. Have the hot grease just as deep as the timbale iron. Be careful to let the batter come within one-fourth inch of the top. Keep mold hot enough to sizzle. If too hot the timbale slips off, or if too cold it will stick.

Put mold into the grease and heat gradually when ready to cook. Have grease hot but not smoking. This will make three dozen. Use a small saucepan deep enough for the grease to boil up without running over.

Individual Apple Pies

Make tart shells the size desired, baking over bottoms of patty pans (see tart shells). Fill with cold apple sauce, sweetened and seasoned. Top with whipped cream, or garnish with a rosette of mashed and seasoned cottage or Philadelphia cream cheese.

Individual Peach Pie

Make tart shells, fill with canned peaches, or fresh ones, sliced thin and sweetened. Cover top with whipped cream, jelly meringue or cheese.

Lemon Tarts

Juice and grated rind of 2 lemons. Grate 2 sponge cakes (2 large lady-fingers).

Beat 2 eggs light and add one cup of sugar. Mix all together. Mix rich pastry, line patty pans and fill with mixture. Bake.

This makes about 9 tarts in muffin pans.

Chess Tarts

Make small shells. For filling use Janet's Chess Pie. (See recipe in Pies.)

Cheese Straws

2 cups flour	⅛ teaspoon cayenne pepper
1 cup grated cheese	Ice-cold water to make very stiff
1 teaspoon salt	dry dough
Butter the size of an egg	

Mix salt, pepper and butter into the flour, add cheese and mix with the ice water. Cover and place in ice box for 30 minutes, roll out, fold and roll again. Repeat this four times. Roll out to ¼ inch thickness, cut in ¼ inch strips about 4 inches long, place on baking sheet and bake in moderate oven until a light, crisp brown.

Sometimes cut small biscuit about as large as a half dollar and bake as crackers or wafers. The oven should be very hot when put in, then reduced to medium heat.

PIES

My Favorite Lemon Pie

1 cup sugar	3 tablespoons of sugar for the
1 cup of wet light bread	meringue
3 eggs	Butter the size of an egg
Juice of 1 large lemon	

Remove the crust from fresh bread and dip into a bowl of water until it will take up enough to be wet thoroughly. Squeeze out the water and measure in a cup—not packing too tight. Put the wet bread, sugar, yolks of eggs, lemon juice and butter into a double boiler and cook until thick

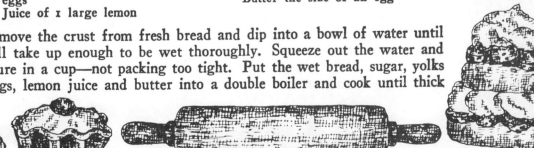

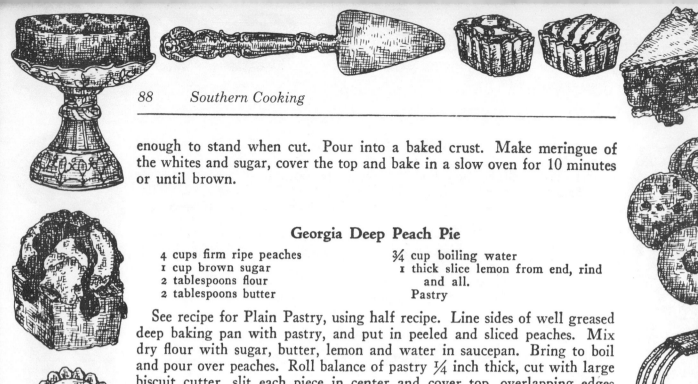

enough to stand when cut. Pour into a baked crust. Make meringue of the whites and sugar, cover the top and bake in a slow oven for 10 minutes or until brown.

Georgia Deep Peach Pie

4 cups firm ripe peaches
1 cup brown sugar
2 tablespoons flour
2 tablespoons butter

¾ cup boiling water
1 thick slice lemon from end, rind and all.
Pastry

See recipe for Plain Pastry, using half recipe. Line sides of well greased deep baking pan with pastry, and put in peeled and sliced peaches. Mix dry flour with sugar, butter, lemon and water in saucepan. Bring to boil and pour over peaches. Roll balance of pastry ¼ inch thick, cut with large biscuit cutter, slit each piece in center and cover top, overlapping edges but leaving spaces for steam to escape. Bake in moderate oven 40 minutes until fruit is juicy done and pastry brown.

Peach Pie or Cobbler

4 cups of firm sliced peaches
1 cup sugar
¼ cup water

Enough pastry for a deep baking dish or pie plate

Slice peaches in usual slices, moderately thick. Make a syrup of the sugar and water; boil for three minutes; turn the peaches into the syrup and cook gently until tender. While peaches are cooking prepare the pastry, using two cups of flour. Line sides of baking dish or pan with pastry; lift the peaches out and line the bottom of dish; dot with butter and a dusting of flour; repeat until all is used. Pour on the juice and cover top with pastry, same as making pie. Make generous opening in top of center; cook in moderate oven 30 to 40 minutes. For the usual pie make same as blackberry.

Cherry Pie

2½ cups flour
1 teaspoon salt

8 tablespoons cold, firm shortening
6 tablespoons ice-cold water

Make as directed in pastry for shell. Divide into two pieces, roll out thin (as thick as the tine of a silver fork), put into pan, press firmly over all parts. Brush top side of the bottom (not sides) with melted grease. Put in filling, wet edge with cold water.

Roll out top and place over pie, press edges together well, trim and crimp edge with a fork. Make generous opening in top and pie is ready to go into oven.

Bake on or near bottom of oven, have oven hot, reduce to medium heat, bake 30 to 40 minutes.

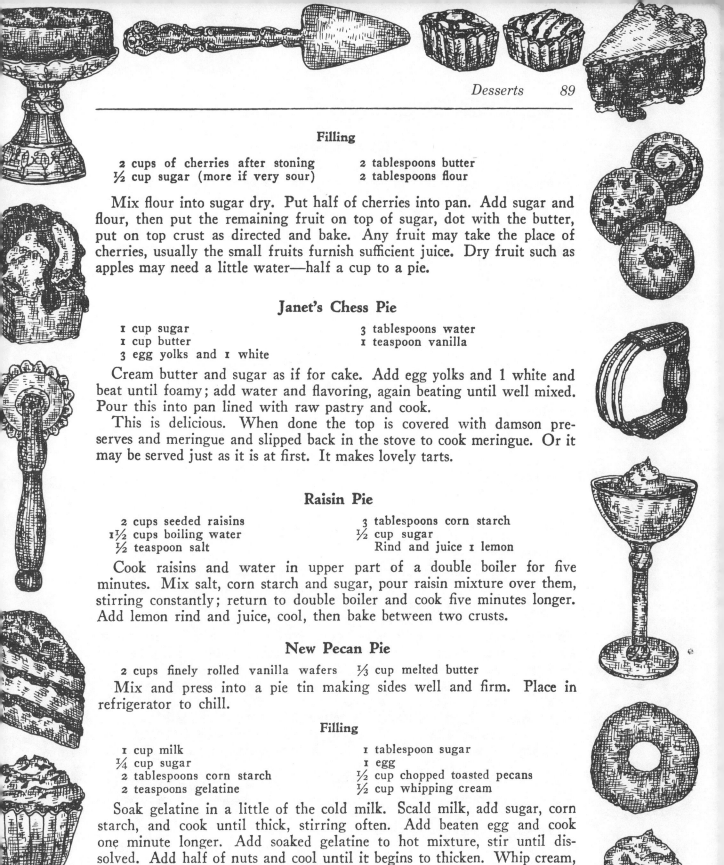

Filling

2 cups of cherries after stoning
½ cup sugar (more if very sour)
2 tablespoons butter
2 tablespoons flour

Mix flour into sugar dry. Put half of cherries into pan. Add sugar and flour, then put the remaining fruit on top of sugar, dot with the butter, put on top crust as directed and bake. Any fruit may take the place of cherries, usually the small fruits furnish sufficient juice. Dry fruit such as apples may need a little water—half a cup to a pie.

Janet's Chess Pie

1 cup sugar
1 cup butter
3 egg yolks and 1 white
3 tablespoons water
1 teaspoon vanilla

Cream butter and sugar as if for cake. Add egg yolks and 1 white and beat until foamy; add water and flavoring, again beating until well mixed. Pour this into pan lined with raw pastry and cook.

This is delicious. When done the top is covered with damson preserves and meringue and slipped back in the stove to cook meringue. Or it may be served just as it is at first. It makes lovely tarts.

Raisin Pie

2 cups seeded raisins
1½ cups boiling water
½ teaspoon salt
3 tablespoons corn starch
½ cup sugar
Rind and juice 1 lemon

Cook raisins and water in upper part of a double boiler for five minutes. Mix salt, corn starch and sugar, pour raisin mixture over them, stirring constantly; return to double boiler and cook five minutes longer. Add lemon rind and juice, cool, then bake between two crusts.

New Pecan Pie

2 cups finely rolled vanilla wafers   ⅓ cup melted butter

Mix and press into a pie tin making sides well and firm. Place in refrigerator to chill.

Filling

1 cup milk
¼ cup sugar
2 tablespoons corn starch
2 teaspoons gelatine
1 tablespoon sugar
1 egg
½ cup chopped toasted pecans
½ cup whipping cream

Soak gelatine in a little of the cold milk. Scald milk, add sugar, corn starch, and cook until thick, stirring often. Add beaten egg and cook one minute longer. Add soaked gelatine to hot mixture, stir until dissolved. Add half of nuts and cool until it begins to thicken. Whip cream, add sugar (1 tablespoon) and add to milk mixture folding in. Pour into chilled crust. Sprinkle top with remainder of chopped pecans and let chill thoroughly. Serve.

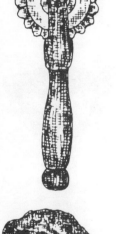

Crepe Suzettes

Use popover batter for crepe. Into a moderately hot, large, heavy fry pan or skillet, about 9 or 10 inches across, put 2 tablespoons of cooking oil—pour in just enough batter to cover the bottom well, turning pan from side to side to cover almost the entire surface, cook until bottom is lightly browned, turn to cook top side, using a spatula or pancake turner. When done fold in half, then in quarter, place on platter until enough are made, then place each folded pancake in the suzette (sauce), cook over gentle heat until well saturated. Place on platter and pour over the remaining sauce. If brandy or liquors are used, California brandy and rum are preferable, the quantity to be determined by the individual.

Sauce for Crepe Suzettes

1 cup sugar	1 grated orange rind
2 tablespoons butter	1 cup orange juice

Melt and cook together until consistency of syrup. Several liqueurs may be added for seasoning if desired.

Baked Alaska
First Part

5 egg whites	10 tablespoons sugar
⅛ teaspoon salt	

Second Part

1 layer of cake	1 piece cardboard
1 quart brick of Neapolitan ice cream	3 pieces writing paper
1 steak plank	

Prepare plank, on this place cardboard, writing paper then cake.

Make meringue, being careful that eggs are fresh, and the meringue very stiff, beating after all sugar is in until smooth, glossy and stiff.

Place brick of cream on cake; having cake 1 inch larger all around. Cover generously with meringue—using about half. Put the remaining portion in forcing bag (this bag must be of rubber) with star tube, and decorate the loaf in any fancy way desired—making it very high and full in rosettes and peaks. Sprinkle well with sugar (about 1 tablespoon—this is extra). Have oven very hot (about 500 degrees), lower rack so the top of meringue will be just above the center. Place plank and all into oven, bake with hot fire (about 2 minutes) until the meringue is a delicate brown, and darker brown on the high points. Watch closely, remove, slip white paper, top layer and all on a platter.

Serve at once. Slice through meringue, ice cream and cake.

The dish is prettier if garnished with cherries, crystallized rose leaves or violets.

Sponge or butter cake may be used.

Individual Alaska

Use rounds of cake, placing on this ice cream in ball shape (using round ice cream scoop) and putting the meringue on in any way preferred. Bake same as the large Alaska.

Forcing Bag and Tube

The pastry tube is a small tin tube with a star or round shaped end which forms the shape of the icing or meringue. The bag is entirely separate, but the two must be put together to use either. For icing, meringue, creams and mayonnaise, you should have a rubber bag made of rubber sheeting. A 12-inch square sewed on the machine into a three-cornered bag, the small end cut large enough for the tin tube to extend out, the bag filled and mixture piped through the tube which forms fancy shapes. For potatoes or anything hot make bag of a piece of heavy unbleached drilling and use the same way. Hot potatoes would ruin the rubber. The tube can be purchased at any hardware store for ten cents, or so much per set, of many shapes. Sometimes the bag can be purchased. They can be made much cheaper. There are metal containers that come with the tubes if desired.

DUMPLINGS AND SHORTCAKES

Apple Dumplings

⅓ cup shortening	1 egg
¾ cup sweet milk	1 tablespoon sugar
1 teaspoon salt	Flour enough to make soft dough
4 teaspoons baking powder	

Roll dough ¼ inch thick, cover with slices of apple, chopped slightly, and bits of butter; roll like a jelly roll and cut in pieces about 1½ inch thick; drop into boiling sauce and bake 30 to 40 minutes.

The Sauce

1 cup sugar	4 tablespoons butter, cinnamon
3 cups boiling water	or nutmeg
4 tablespoons sifted flour	

Mix flour dry with sugar; add butter and then hot water; let come to the boil; put dumplings down in the sauce on the cut end and cook in sauce; sprinkle nutmeg over the top. This dumpling is good baked dry and served with hard sauce. This will make 12 large dumplings.

Apple Pudding

Peel and slice apples as for a pie, put in a layer of apples, bits of butter, sugar to sweeten, and a sprinkle of flour (about 1 teaspoon), fill a pan half full, having apple about 2 inches deep. Make a batter as follows:

1 egg	1 teaspoon vanilla
½ cup sugar	3 teaspoons baking powder
½ cup sweet milk	1 cup flour
2 tablespoons of melted butter (or oil)	Pinch of salt

Mix as for cake; pour over the apples. Bake in moderate oven 30 to 40 minutes. Serve with hard sauce or whipped cream. This will serve six. When turned out the apples are on top.

Apple Torte

2 eggs	1½ teaspoons baking powder
1 cup sugar	⅛ teaspoon salt
½ cup chopped nuts	1 teaspoon vanilla
3½ tablespoons flour	1 cup chopped apples

Beat eggs well, add other ingredients and mix. Bake in shallow greased pan half an hour at 350 degrees. Serve with whipped cream.

Peach Cobbler

For a family of six, use 3 cups of firm peaches, sliced in the usual way, having them of medium thickness. Use 1 cup of sugar, ¼ cup of water, bring to a boil and let boil for a few seconds. Add peaches and simmer slowly while making the pastry.

Line sides of pan or baking dish with pastry. Carefully lift out peaches and form a layer on bottom, dot with butter, put another layer until all is used. Cover top with pastry, make a generous slash in center both ways, bake in moderate oven 30 to 40 minutes.

If peaches are very acid, use more sugar.

Often a sprinkling of flour may be placed after each layer of peaches—this rather thickens the liquor and is liked by many. A layer of pastry may be put between each layer of peaches if liked.

Peach Melba Shortcake

2 cups fresh peaches, or equal of canned	½ cup 4x sugar
½ cup sugar	1 cup thick cream whipped and sweetened or a jelly meringue
1 pint raspberries	

Peel and slice thin, ripe peaches, cover with sugar for an hour. Crush raspberries, add sugar. Make the usual shortcake dough, open, butter and spread with peaches, then raspberries. Put on top layer, repeat. Cover top with whipped cream or meringue. Cut individual shortcakes with large biscuit cutter.

Cranberry Shortcake

1 cup ground raw cranberries	⅓ cup grated (or crushed) pineapple
1 cup grated apples	
1 small bottle red cherries	1 cup sugar

Grind and measure cranberries, also red cherries. Mix all together and let stand several hours. Make the usual rich biscuit shortcake dough, baking in two layers. Separate layers, spread with the mixture, putting together like a layer cake. Cover the top with the fruit mixture and cover again with whipped cream or jelly meringue. Serve immediately. The dough is made same as for strawberry shortcake.

New Shortcake

6 egg whites (unbeaten)	½ teaspoon cream tartar
2 cups granulated sugar	1 teaspoon vanilla

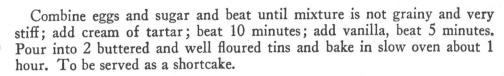

Combine eggs and sugar and beat until mixture is not grainy and very stiff; add cream of tartar; beat 10 minutes; add vanilla, beat 5 minutes. Pour into 2 buttered and well floured tins and bake in slow oven about 1 hour. To be served as a shortcake.

Strawberry Shortcake

⅓ cup shortening
¾ cup sweet milk
1 egg
2½ cups flour

1 teaspoon salt
4 teaspoons baking powder
1 tablespoon sugar

Put all dry ingredients together and sift. Mix shortening into the flour, put egg into milk and mix together and make into a dough. Turn on a floured board and knead until smooth.

Divide in two parts, pat or roll out to fit a pie pan, sprinkle generously with flour, roll out second piece and place on top. Bake in moderate oven until well done (about 30 minutes). Separate the layers, spread generously with soft butter. Have ready a box of berries sliced and sweetened. Spread the berries over the layer (half of them), then put the top layer on and more berries on top.

Cover the whole with whipped cream or jelly meringue, and serve. Use about ¾ of a cup of sugar to a box of berries.

Willie's Strawberry Pie

1 cup of ripe berries cut
  in half
1 medium size baked pie shell
1 cup crushed berries

½ cup sugar
1 tablespoon corn starch
½ cup heavy cream
Few grains salt

Halve and measure one cup of ripe strawbrerries, and put into baked pie shell.

Crush and measure one cup of ripe strawberries, heat to boiling, add 1 cup sugar, 2 tablespoons corn starch, and few grains of salt. Cook five minutes. Cool and pour over berries in pie shell. Put in refrigerator for two hours before serving. Heap with whipped cream when ready to serve.

Jelly Meringue

½ glass of firm jelly
1 egg white

Pinch of salt

Into a bowl place all ingredients and with a good egg whip begin to beat just as though you were whipping cream or eggs. Keep beating until quite stiff and it will hold its shape. Use same as whipped cream.

Index